The Call to Unite

The
Call to Unite

∽

Voices of Hope and Awakening

EDITED BY

Tim Shriver AND Tom Rosshirt

THE OPEN FIELD · PENGUIN LIFE

VIKING
An imprint of Penguin Random House LLC
penguinrandomhouse.com

The Open Field/A Penguin Life Book

LIBRARY OF CONGRESS CATALOGING-IN-PUBLICATION DATA

Names: Shriver, Timothy, editor. | Rosshirt, Tom, editor.
Title: The call to unite : voices of hope and awakening /
edited by Tim Shriver and Tom Rosshirt.
Description: New York : Viking, 2021.
Identifiers: LCCN 2020043049 (print) | LCCN 2020043050 (ebook) |
ISBN 9780593298237 (hardcover) | ISBN 9780593298244 (ebook)
Subjects: LCSH: Resilience (Personality trait) | Persistence. |
Affirmations. | Conduct of life.
Classification: LCC BF698.35.R47 C364 2021 (print) |
LCC BF698.35.R47 (ebook) | DDC 158–dc23
LC record available at https://lccn.loc.gov/2020043049
LC ebook record available at https://lccn.loc.gov/2020043050

Printed in the United States of America
1   3   5   7   9   10   8   6   4   2

DESIGNED BY MEIGHAN CAVANAUGH

~

Dear Reader,

The Open Field will commission and publish voices from all walks of life and areas of human endeavor that seek to inform, ignite, inspire, and move humanity forward—one person at a time.

The Open Field books are unique in look and feel, in mission and purpose. Each one is meant to carry your mind beyond judgments and troubles, into new reaches of peace and compassion.

You can expect inspiration and authenticity from The Open Field. You can trust that a book from this imprint will make a difference in your life and in your heart.

With gratitude,
Maria

~

To the prophets and dreamers dismissed as traitors

for seeing unity in humanity

I am convinced that men hate each other because they fear each other. They fear each other because they don't know each other, and they don't know each other because they don't communicate with each other, and they don't communicate with each other because they are separated from each other.

—Reverend Martin Luther King Jr., in a speech delivered at Cornell College on October 15, 1962

Let's invite the world to unite!

—Meisha Lerato Robinson, cofounder, UNITE

Contents

✑

I. Love in the Madness

STORIES OF THE PANDEMIC

II. Pain Always Leaves a Gift

INSIGHTS FOR PERSONAL CHANGE

III. Magic Enters the Room

STORIES AND PRACTICES OF TRANSFORMATION

IV. No Boundaries Are Real

SEEING UNITY IN HUMANITY

V. Our Only Chance to Triumph

LOVE IN ACTION

VI. Renew the Face of the Earth

A CALL TO LOVE

Foreword

Tim Shriver

⁓

Over the course of my life, I've seen again and again how people flourish when they unite, and how they suffer when they're separate. I saw it when I taught high school, where membership in a club helped my students resist the allure of gangs. I've seen it in the movement for social and emotional learning, where kids who learn empathy give up bullying for belonging. I've seen it as chair of Special Olympics, where athletes who've been isolated their whole lives shine with joy when they come together.

But the most striking lesson I've learned about belonging I learned from watching Special Olympics volunteers, including myself. Year after year, we come to help and we get humbled—because we think we're coming to serve "the broken people," and *we* are the ones who are made whole.

My teacher Richard Rohr clarified this mystery for me. The people on the margins of any group hold the secret to the wholeness of that very group, he said, because as soon as we stop pushing people out and start letting them in, *we* become whole.

Every one of us is eager to be part of some circle that excludes us. We want to be in the in-group and flee the out-group. We want to be with *these* people and separate from *those* people. So, we seek belonging for ourselves by *denying* it to others. And that's exactly backward. We get belonging by giving it.

The most joyful people I've ever met—the people I revere and want to be like—seem to carry their belonging inside them. They are never trying to push their way in. They're never trying to force anyone out. They don't see themselves as separate. They're not trying to be superior. They open up and take everyone in. That is what it means to unite—and to be a uniter. Uniters do not expect uniformity of opinion, but do seek unity in treating others with dignity—which gives justice a chance to flourish.

We need more uniters now, because we're caught in a crisis of division. Division is not the same as disagreement, and it's not simply the belief that I can do better if you do worse. It's the belief that you *have to do worse* for me to do better. This belief can poison any demographic difference we have, whether it's rich/poor, black/white, Muslim/Christian, conservative/liberal, or urban/rural.

Unfortunately, we all have an urge to divide. It's an instinct born of fear. We have to work hard to overcome it, but some leaders in media and politics don't want us to overcome it; they want to exploit it. They get more viewers and voters and dollars and followers if we're divided, so they turn us against each other, filling our brains with the message: "Those people are 'the other.' They're not like us. They're beneath us. They hate us. They want to hurt us."

The dividers are telling us to *stay* divided, that life is better and safer if we're separate. They've been selling us this story since the dawn of time, and they've had all of history to prove it. But they can't—because their story is a lie. We are one, and when we act as one we can work miracles.

It's not that our differences aren't real or don't matter. Many of our differences make us special, unique—a gift to the whole. Our stories, our cultures, our histories all deserve their place. But underneath our differences, we have common needs and dreams that bind us, that we can fulfill only through each other.

This is not just an act of faith, it's a fact of science. Unity is reality. Like gravity. We either honor the truth and prosper, or defy the truth and suffer.

In 2019, a group of us gathered to form UNITE, to promote a culture where we cross lines that divide us and work on ideas that unite us.

As we began to face the crisis of division, the world was hit with a crisis of disease, and as the virus began to spread, much of the world said, "Oh, that's over there. That doesn't affect me." Now there isn't a person in the world who hasn't been affected by this pandemic—by the sickness from it, by the suffering from it, by the fear from it.

The pandemic is brutally suited to making us see we're connected. If more people around us are healthy, we're more likely to stay healthy. If more people around us are sick, we're more likely to get sick. What I do affects you. What you do affects me. We depend on each other.

Many of us are saying that the virus brought us together, and in some cases it's true. But in other cases, the virus split us apart. And that's been instructive, because in places where we were united, we did better, and in areas where we were divided, we did worse. The virus makes the case in a way almost nothing else ever has: the only way to win is to unite.

In March 2020, just before the lockdowns were announced in the United States, UNITE cofounder Meisha Lerato Robinson returned to Washington, DC, from a road trip through the South, where she had gone to meet people and talk deeply with them. She felt that what the media was telling us about each other was wrong, that the reality was different, and better. She met with everyone from a Cracker Barrel waitress to a survivor of domestic abuse to a Tuskegee Airman and asked each one, "Who do people think you are, and who are you really?" Every person opened up and told her their stories, and Meisha Lerato came to feel that there is more pain in people than we know, and more love and hope there, too. It was one of the most inspiring and unifying experiences of her life. Back in DC, though, she felt the fear of the virus taking hold in the city and in herself, and thought, "Maybe if we open up to each other, we can help each other through this." So she said to her colleagues, "This virus is making us isolate. Let's invite the world to unite!"

This became our first major project, and it forced us to face the question, *How can we move from a culture that divides us to a culture that unites us?* Human beings are an imitative species; we tend to reproduce what we see and hear. If we're going to change our culture, we have to change what we're hearing. So, we thought about all the people we wanted to listen to, all the people we look up to—and we gathered them together for twenty-four hours.

Nuns and priests, nurses and doctors, singers and actors, dancers and writers, monks and ministers, store clerks and truck drivers, ex-presidents and ex-cons— the grieving, the hopeful, the heartbroken—all came together to share stories and lessons about what hurts and what helps, who we love and what we've lost, telling the truth about our needs, our fears, and our most audacious dreams.

In the pages of this book, we capture many of those moments. We hear Jacqui Lewis say we are Houses of God; Charlamagne say we have to tell our stories; Shaka Senghor say we have to give ourselves grace. We hear Deepak Chopra say no boundaries are real, and Rev. angel say we should look at the sky.

Martin Luther King III called for a revolution of values. TD Jakes said we've become too tribal. Arthur Brooks said the answer is love. President

Bush said we're determined to rise. And Rick Warren appealed to people in despair, saying, "We need you alive."

Three weeks later, George Floyd was dead.

Black men and women have been killed by police countless times, but this time a vast range of people—from political activists to first-time protestors—pulled together across racial lines, socioeconomic lines, and generational lines to mount the most unified protests for racial justice in the history of the United States.

I asked Reverend Jen Bailey what made this moment new. "We were all physically limited by the pandemic," she said. "So we were able to pay a different sort of attention. And hearing George Floyd call out for his mother in his last moments—knowing as we did that his mother had passed away years before—revealed the cruelty at the core of his death, and prompted us to respond in the most humane way, which is to speak out and demand something different."

Father Greg Boyle, who founded the world's largest gang intervention and rehabilitation organization, told me, "Spiritual evolution means coming to see the wholeness of the person—as God sees—and this is the compassionate seeing that these events have awakened. That's why the movement has gained so much traction, and that's why the face of the protest is so diverse. It seems to embody our deepest longing to be in this together."

Is this an awakening? If it is, and I believe it is, then we're going to begin solving crises everywhere. Our crisis of racial injustice is older than our country and pervasive in our history. It is tied to the crisis of division; it is tied to the crisis of disease; and it is tied to every crisis to come, because the crises we refuse to solve persist for the same reason. The dividers always blame "the other"—and we won't ever end this until the "the other" is us.

That defines the choice in every crisis. Divide or unite. Blame the other or *become* the other. Until now, too many of us have chosen to divide. But something new is happening. Rising numbers of people now refuse to be othered and refuse to other, refuse to be dominated and refuse to dominate. That's a shock to the culture. It's creating a sense of upheaval that wasn't there before, and that's a good sign. Change never comes in calm times. Change comes in times of crisis, when we see the way we're living isn't working.

We're tired of hostility. We're starving for unity. We're telling a new story of who we are. We are all connected as one people. We find joy in each other's joy. We find purpose in each other's happiness. We find belonging without excluding. We seek forgiveness through forgiving. We find our identity without othering. We feel called to unite.

The call to unite is not an event. It's not a book. It doesn't belong to a group. It's a voice sounding inside of us. In every crisis, if we listen to our hearts, we can hear the call to unite. It's what invites us to hope. It's what guides us to love. It's what sustains us on the journey to justice.

It's a long path to overcome our past. We live with the legacy of a world that didn't know we are one. But we now see more clearly what they saw "through a glass darkly": None of us can survive on our own. Not one of us can be happy alone. We need each other. Now more than ever.

The Call to Unite

I.

Love in the Madness

STORIES OF THE PANDEMIC

One of the most loving gifts we can offer each other is a story of how we feel when we've lost control of our lives. In these pages on the pandemic, people share the crisis through their eyes, and they show us that the best way to summon love is to say bravely and openly: "My heart is broken."

Nurses helping patients, store clerks selling food, drivers bringing supplies, principals running schools, and emergency room physicians at safety-net hospitals serving those with nothing—they all stood guard over the dignity of those in need, and they showed us the love and courage of human beings in crisis.

Many of them were moved to do more for others than they had ever done before, no matter the risk, regardless of the cost. They proved that we can

Medical workers comfort each other outside Severo Ochoa Hospital. Leganes, Spain. March 2020.

reach the highest ideal of who we hope to be—treating everyone like they matter, leaving no one out, loving people we don't even know. They lifted our sights and left us thinking, "I want to be like them."

These scenes of humanity move us toward unity. Even adversaries come together when they see things they both love. And who doesn't love seeing human beings braving their fears to serve those who suffer? It doesn't matter what our differences are; we are all moved by that kind of courage.

Writing Goodbye Letters

D'neil Schmall, an ICU nurse, moved to New York City in March 2020 to join the fight against COVID-19. She was part of a rapid response team treating patients at a temporary Central Park hospital.

❧

Coming in as a crisis nurse, you leave your hometown and everything that's familiar. You go in to work. You come back to your hotel. There's nothing in between. There are no comforts of home. I'd been here for a week and a half, running on four hours of sleep a night, doing seventeen-hour shifts, and then I had a terrible day. I was injured at work. A couple of my patients passed. Then I walked into another patient's room and he was deceased, and I bottled it all in. On the way home, I started sobbing to my Uber driver, saying, "I don't think people understand how stressful this job is." And he said, "How would we know if no one ever tells us?"

When I got back to my hotel, I sobbed on the floor for another two hours as I was writing goodbye letters to my mother and my sister and my aunt. I said everything I have ever wanted to say or apologize for in my lifetime. And then I decided to post a video saying everything that was on my mind. I never thought I would have to deal with the outcome of that video because I didn't think I would be alive to see it. But I did it in the hope that even if it didn't happen in my lifetime, maybe it could change the industry for the people I work with. The response has been amazing. I have been contacted by people all over the world. I think they are now aware that health-care workers go through things just as our patients do, and we feel for them and we take them on as a reflection of our job. We want to do a good job and what happens to our patients—sometimes we take that to heart. Even though we have done everything we could, we carry that grief with us.

I'm FaceTiming Their Families While They're Dying

Jeanette Jackson-Gaines, Dawn Feldthouse, and Michael Merritt are nurses in New York City.

⌒

JEANETTE: I never thought in my lifetime or my children's lifetimes or my grandchildren's lifetimes that I would see this. I'm used to taking care of patients who are critically ill, who require a lot, but this is above and beyond. Most of the patients I've taken care of have comorbidities, which put them at a higher risk. But some of them are young, and are still going down this horrific road. It's tough. It's anxiety ridden. Most nights I don't sleep. I'm lying awake, thinking about going back into the battlefield, taking care of patients.

DAWN: This pandemic is pushing us to our limits, and I have broken down in tears many times. One of the hardest things has been knowing that our COVID patients are often alone in these isolation rooms, unable to have visitors. At NYU Langone, we formed a team that goes around with iPads to help our patients see their families. In one of my darkest moments, I came home in tears, wishing there was more I could do. That was the moment I created the Join the Fight Against COVID campaign in support of our frontline heroes. We needed more PPE, more masks, more gowns. We needed housing for thousands of nurses coming in from all over. As the gifts came in, they were accompanied with an outpouring of love. As I read through all of those notes, I could see the support that was always there. In my little loop of going into the COVID units, going into the isolation units, going home, trying to get some sleep and then waking up the next day to do it all over again, there was a disconnect—I wasn't aware of all these people who wanted to help and were already helping. Their support gave me the courage and inspiration to keep going in.

MICHAEL: I've been an emergency room trauma nurse for twenty-three years. In normal times, we see more tragedy in a year than most people see in a lifetime. But over the past several weeks, I've seen more tragedy than I've seen in my whole career. I walk into work and there is a roomful of people on ventilators. I walk into another area and there's another group of people on ventilators. And I don't care how bad the flu season gets, I don't care how bad H1N1 was; we *never, ever* had so many patients long term on ventilators. That's not what we're used to. We're ER nurses. We treat them. We street them. We're ready for the next patients. But now we've become ICU nurses because these patients don't go anywhere. They stay on the ventilators for weeks at a time.

I have patients who pass away and I'm the only one in the room. I'm FaceTiming their families while they're dying. And it's not like the family is in California; they're outside our hospital. I've cried more times than I think I've ever cried as a nurse. I've cried with families. I've cried with staff members. It takes an emotional toll. And I consider us tough ER nurses and tough ICU nurses, and it still hurts. I wake up in the middle of the night and I hear ventilator alarms, and I hear monitor alarms, or I'm in a panic thinking, *Do I have a fever?*

It's hard, but what gives me hope is humanity coming together to help. I want to thank the restaurant that's donating food for health-care workers, and the physicians at Bellevue getting people hotel rooms so they don't have to go home and risk infecting their families.

I work with a nurse who's retired, and she said, "I just couldn't not come." I want to thank all the nurses who packed their bags, left their families, and risked their health to come help us on the front lines. We're here every single day, and it hurts deeply. But it gives us hope that they came here to help.

Healing the Human Beings

Kate Judge is the executive director of the American Nurses Foundation.

ᘓ

N urses are doing heroic, courageous, frightening work, but it has been too big a request. They're getting support from their peers, but their peers are overwhelmed, too. They get some help from their families, but many aren't living with their families. When we get to the other side, they're going to need help to recover from the trauma. The human toll of this pandemic has been great, and healing the human beings at the center of it will be critical.

Building the RH60 Ventilator Machine

Trevar Smedal is a machinist for GE Healthcare. He is a member of the International Association of Machinists and Aerospace Workers— Local 1406 in Madison, Wisconsin.

ᘓ

I work every day building the RH60 ventilator machine, the machine people get hooked up to when they have difficulties breathing due to this virus. Since this pandemic came out, a lot has changed on our line as far as the number of machines we need to get out and how many employees we have. We're constantly getting new employees so we can build an adequate num-

A family speaks to a hospitalized loved one. New Delhi, India.
July 2020.

ber of machines, so we have to be thoughtful about how to train them while keeping everything safe and building a quality product.

We had three of our members go out for health reasons, and when some of your team members go out and don't come back it's hard to maintain camaraderie on the line and continue to build. But I know why I answer the call every morning when I wake up and go to work. My sister is a doctor in Cincinnati, and she has to fight this virus on the front lines. My job is to help her and all the other medical professionals in the world because they're the frontline fighters, and I'm going to continue to build quality medical products until this pandemic is finally over.

I Love You. I Love You. I Love You. I'm Going to Have the Breathing Tube Put in Now.

Drs. Lakshmana Swamy (Boston Medical Center), Dara Kass (Columbia University Medical Center), and Steven McDonald (NYU Langone Medical Center) are emergency medical specialists. Enrico Poletti is a cardiology resident in Milan, Italy.

ᕮ

LAKSHMANA: My hospital is a safety-net hospital. We take care of some of the most disenfranchised people in the region. It's terrifying to see the statistics because it is just a further separation between who has and who has not. The racial disparities can't be overstated. We have a lot of patients coming in with severe cases of COVID. I'm seeing the extreme, and yet the hospital is unnaturally quiet.

Normally, our ICUs are full of patients and families and staff. People are congregating at the nursing station. The doors are all open. We're going in and out of the rooms, engaging with patients and families. And part of what gives us so much energy in our normal intensive-care work is being there for people, holding a patient's hand, talking to families at length. What's hard now is that the personal touch has broken down. Everything is done over FaceTime. It's hard to get in the room. We are distancing even from each other.

We are used to people suffering and dying; that is part of everyday life for us. But this is different. So many people are on ventilators. So many people are on the edge of death—with us hovering like hawks trying to catch every little thing we can to pull people back and get them better. And we take that home with us. It's a level of stress that I haven't experienced before—watching a young parent call her kids at home to say, "I love you, I love you, I love you, I'm going to have the breathing tube put in now."

Not so long ago I went running after a string of shifts, and tears just started pouring down my face. That is not me. That has never happened before. I didn't even know where it was coming from. I think we are seeing a different level of emotional and physical trauma, and the uncertainty affects all of us. Is it going to get to me? Is it going to get my family? How long is it going to last? That fear of the unknown is so profound. It reminds me that the strongest thing we have when we're faced with this fear and we're terrified at night is to come together and support each other however we can.

DARA: I'm a mom. I have three kids, and I had to separate from them when this all started. And that left me with a void from the beginning. So I threw myself into patient care. Then at night I would get scared and cry. That happened in the hospital as well, especially when I had a patient who looked like me—who was a fortysomething parent who was breathing superfast, and her saturation was superlow, and I would get overwhelmed thinking that this could have been my sister, it could have been my husband, it could have been me.

And then I became a coronavirus patient myself. When the virus hit New York City, it came like a tidal wave, so a lot of us who were taking care of patients in the ER caught the virus ourselves. That's not something we normally deal with—our own mortality. I think we are actually learning how to be better doctors through this. We are learning how to humanize our own experience. In the training I went through almost twenty years ago, we didn't identify with our patients. We didn't want to feel too connected. Those of us who did were told to stop. I think at this moment, because the virus is affecting our own families and our personal health, we are much closer to our patients, and every barrier we put up gets broken down.

STEVEN: As the virus was coming, I had extreme anxiety. I felt like I was standing on the shore watching a tsunami on its way. When it hit, the emergency room felt like a wild animal had been let loose from its cage and we were all trying to put it back in. There was a level of freneticism I've never seen in my career as an emergency room physician.

But what is really weighing on me is the disproportionate impact this is having on communities of color, on immigrant communities, on our most disenfranchised Americans. I have been trying to channel that anxiety and stress by writing, by trying to be an advocate, by having conversations—doing things that really can help raise awareness about the disparities we're seeing.

ENRICO: At the beginning, I actually felt excited because for the first time in my short career I felt useful. But now when I come home from the hospital what I feel most is frustration, because I see so many people suffering. They're just on their own. I can do so few things. I was not ready for that.

The principal source of stress for me is watching patients struggle alone. And it's not only COVID patients, but every patient in the hospital is completely isolated now, and we need to give them some strength. I'll tell you an example. One of our patients was going on ventilation. He had a phone, but the phone ran out of power. We found a charger so he could FaceTime his family, and he was so grateful to us. Unfortunately, two days later he died. His family called us back to thank us because we gave him a chance to say goodbye. I'm not ashamed to say I cried. It was not the only time I cried.

My Stomach Twists and Fingers Shake

Dr. Elizabeth Mitchell is an emergency physician at Boston Medical Center.

ᢩᡒ

I have been writing a lot lately, especially a lot of poetry. Poetry can help doctors be better listeners. It speaks to the art, not the science, of medicine.

Recently, I was moved to write a poem about what it's like to go into an emergency department during COVID.

The idea came to me when I put on personal protective gear for the first time. I remember watching videos to make sure I was doing it right. I had a feeling of dread—like there was a threat to me as a physician, and I know the nurses felt the same way. It was unlike any medical event I had ever experienced.

Then, after a series of shifts, I was out for a walk on a beautiful day, and I saw the flowers blooming, and I thought, the world feels like it's completely shifted, but in another way it feels the same: flowers are still coming up in spring.

Somehow, all the things that were changing and all things that were staying the same came together for me in this poem.

I call it "The Apocalypse."

> This is the apocalypse
> A daffodil has poked its head up
> from the dirt and opened
> sunny arms to bluer skies
> yet I am filled with
> dark and anxious dread
> as theaters close as travel ends and
> grocery stores display their empty rows
> where toilet paper liquid bleach
> and bags of flour stood in upright ranks.
> My stomach twists and fingers shake
> as I prepare to work the battleground
> the place I've always loved and felt at home
> is now a field of droplets sprayed across a room
> or lurking on a handle or a sink to find their way
> inside our trusting hands or mouths or eyes
> the ones that touch you when you're sick

speak soothing words and seek the answer to your pain.
This is the apocalypse
as spring begins again
and brightly colored flowers
deploy in my backyard
the neighbors walk their dogs
and march along the quiet streets
I stretch my purple gloves on steady hands
I tie my yellow gown behind my back
my hair inside a blue bouffant
my mouth and nose and eyes are
still and calm inside their waiting shields.
This is the apocalypse.

May I Be a Source of Healing

Naomi Judd is a Grammy Award–winning country music singer and actress.

ᴄ𝄐

Before my singing career, I was a registered nurse in the intensive care unit. On one of my first days, the supervisor came to me and said she had a patient fresh out of the operating room. Her leg had been amputated, and she didn't have any family or friends with her. The supervisor asked me to be there when she woke up, and to tell her that she had lost her leg. I found out right away that taking care of patients is not just about skills and training; it's also about loving-kindness.

That's what I think about when I see the nurses and doctors putting on PPE, wearing it for a whole shift with their backs hurt and their feet sore, working in one of the most dangerous places on earth, knowing they could take the virus home to their families.

Here's a gift I would like to give them—a meditation that I used to use every day that I was in the unit: "May I be at peace. May my heart remain open. May I awaken to the light of my own true nature. May I be healed. May I be a source of healing for others."

Please be safe. We care about you. We love you.

Won't Stop Me from Doing My Job

Dale Pink is a UPS driver in Delaware and a member of the International Brotherhood of Teamsters—Local 355 in Baltimore, Maryland.

ᢙ

I am putting in long, hard days as a front-line worker, as are all of my fellow UPS teamsters across the country. I'm honored to have been deemed an essential employee. I don't have as much time with my family right now, and I know that every day that I leave my home I'm potentially sacrificing my health and safety, and even my family's. Through my days delivering boxes, I have to be aware of my closeness to other employees and my customers, and I have to remember not to touch my face, and to wash my hands, and to sanitize my truck.

I can't say that these thoughts don't stay with me, but they won't stop me from doing my job. The deliveries I make contain vital supplies like the PPE

Firefighters salute the funeral procession of Edward Singleton,
who died of complications from COVID-19. Chicago, IL,
USA. April 2020.

and the medicines that could save my customers' lives. I'm proud to be doing this job and helping my customers and my country fight this battle. But honestly, I can't wait for this to be over, because my job is a very customer-oriented job. Your customers become your friends, and I miss that, and I miss them, and I miss my coworkers, and most of all, I miss my family.

My Oxygen Levels Plunged

David Lat is a legal recruiter and the founding editor of Above the Law, a legal news website.

I began to feel symptoms in early March. It started with fatigue and loss of taste. After a few days, I started to get fever and chills and aches. Then about a week in, I got a cough and it became hard to breathe. That took me to my local emergency room. I asked for a COVID-19 test, but I hadn't traveled anywhere or interacted with any person known to have it, so I was out of luck. But the next day my breathing was so bad I had a tough time walking, and I came back to the ER, and they admitted me.

They gave me emergency oxygen, my test came back positive, and I was in stable condition for about five days. Then my oxygen levels plunged, and I was put on a ventilator. I remember the intubation briefly. It felt like a scene out of *ER*, or *Chicago Hope*. I felt like there were a million people in the room, even though there were only probably three or four. The last thing I remember was getting the sedation through an IV. I can't recall anything after that, and I'm glad I can't because a lot of people have PTSD or ICU delirium. I remember nothing. I think I like it that way.

Luckily, after six days, I came off the ventilator. Not everybody does. Then I spent another six days in the hospital recovering, getting supplemental oxygen, which they gradually tapered, and then I was released. It's been weeks now, and I'm still trying to recover, and that underscores how serious this is. This isn't something that just affects the ill or the elderly. I'm in my forties, relatively healthy. As we start talking about reopening the economy, which I think is very important, we need to be careful. We need to listen to the physicians and public health experts.

Live Your Life

Amanda Kloots, a personal trainer, is a former Radio City Rockette and Broadway dancer. She married Nick Cordero, a Tony-nominated actor, in 2017 and they share a thirteen-month-old son, Elvis.

ᴄ⁓

My husband, Nick Cordero, has been intubated in the ICU since April 1. It's April 30 today. One of the things that I have done to keep my spirits up—it's so hard as his wife not to be by his side—is to play his music. Nick is a Broadway performer and actor and he writes and sings. He just released his first song, "Live Your Life." So every day at 3:00 p.m., I have asked my community on Instagram to play his song, to sing and to dance so loud that Nick will have to wake up because an army of people will be singing his music. This has become a pillar of strength for me.

Even on days when I'm especially low and feeling like the last thing I can do is sing and dance, at three o'clock I put on his song and I immediately feel better. I think of Nick and of how much he would love to know that this is happening around the world. And when he does wake up, when he does open his eyes, when he does have the ability to understand everything that has happened in the month of April for him, he will not believe that he has an army of people behind him sending their love and their care. Until then, I am staying positive by playing his music, knowing that he'll want to hear it. He'll want to hear it.

Nick Cordero died on July 5, 2020, at Cedars-Sinai Medical Center in Los Angeles.

Liquid Gold

Daniel Dae Kim is an actor, director, and producer.

༼

Early in the pandemic, I had the experience of fighting COVID-19. When I recovered, I wanted to find any way that I could to help, and I learned that I was qualified to donate my plasma. Donating plasma is one of the ways being studied to help patients suffering from the virus. The thinking is that the plasma of someone who's recovered contains the antibodies that fight the virus—so by taking plasma from people who have recovered and infusing it into the bodies of people who have not, we might be able to reduce the severity or shorten the duration of the illness.

The donation process can take from forty-five minutes to a couple of hours depending on a number of factors. After they draw your blood, it gets spun through a centrifuge to separate the plasma from your red blood cells, and what comes out is a yellowish gold liquid. Given how valuable this plasma could be, I have heard some people call it liquid gold.

I was eager to donate, but Hawaii wasn't accepting plasma donations at the time, and I didn't want to wait, so I flew to Los Angeles. Donating plasma is something you can do more than once, and I plan to donate again. Not everyone can give in this way, but everyone can give in some way. If we all help however we can, we'll be sharing a common experience—and that's how we're going to pull through.

A Way for a Mother to Show Her Love

Dr. Myriam Sidibe holds a doctorate in public health focused on handwashing. She spearheaded Unilever's handwashing campaign, the largest hygiene behavior-change program in the world.

౿

I have spent the last twenty years of my professional life researching and promoting handwashing with soap. I led the world's largest handwashing program, reaching one billion people in more than thirty countries. Handwashing with soap could be the most important lifesaving act that we take, and today, it is one of the best lines of defense against COVID-19.

Kindergartners practice washing their hands.
Jerusalem, Israel. May 2020.

One thing I know from all my research is that handwashing with soap is seldom practiced. Before COVID-19, we know that the global rate was about 19 percent, which means that four people out of five come out of the bathroom without washing their hands. That's the same whether you are in the US or in the UK or in Africa. And the ability to practice this lifesaving act is hindered by the fact that three billion people around the world do not have water, soap, and a handwashing facility in their homes.

The core of my work now is to try to embed this behavior change so that we do not stop it when COVID-19 ends. So make sure you are regularly washing your hands for twenty seconds with soap, with water, with a lot of bubbles. It's an act of love—a way for a mother to show her love for her kids, and for kids to show love to the elderly.

The Difference Between a Hero and a Victim

Kailash Satyarthi and his colleagues have emancipated more than ninety thousand children in India and, through their work and advocacy, have freed millions more globally. He received the Nobel Peace Prize in 2014 and the Robert F. Kennedy Human Rights Award in 1995. Kerry Kennedy is the current president of Robert F. Kennedy Human Rights.

ᘒ

KERRY: Kailash, is there somebody in particular whose work has moved you during the coronavirus epidemic?

KAILASH: Yes. We realized early on that there was a serious need of masks in the area where we have our center for freed child slaves. I learned that all the children in the center who know stitching, and even those who didn't know, were making small pieces of mask to distribute to the needy people in the area. The children felt compassion and a sense of responsibility to those who are much more needy, and they acted. That was so moving an experience for me—only a few years ago these children were trapped into slavery and sold and bought like animals. And now they're feeling compassion and helping others.

KERRY: As you talk about those children, it reminds me that the difference between a hero and a victim is activism—taking action on behalf of others. That's what those kids are doing. Each of us has a role to play—some big, some small, but every person can make a difference.

KAILASH: Exactly. Humanity has to feel connected. If we are not able to feel the suffering of others as our own suffering and try to alleviate that suffering, we cannot live in peace. I feel there is a need of a deeper sense of loving-kindness and gratitude. The food which is served on my table is cooked by someone. I have to be thankful to that person, but I have to be equally thankful to all those who are responsible for growing that food, the vegetables, cereals, and milk. My gratitude means I have to feel responsible for them, and that connectedness will help in igniting compassion in this new world post-corona.

A Dairy Farmer Who Was
Absolutely in Tears

*Sister Simone Campbell is the leader of Nuns on the Bus, a Catholic
social justice advocacy group. Rabbi Jonah Pesner is the director of the
Religious Action Center of Reform Judaism. Anwar Khan is the
president of Islamic Relief USA.*

∽

SIMONE: Through our organization, we come together in Washington, DC,
with Democrats and Republicans and independents to create policies that
can help solve the crises of our times, and it gives us joy to do this work with
our brothers and sisters from other faiths.

JONAH: Our organization comes out of a tradition that sees itself through
thousands of years of history. Having been liberated from slavery in Egypt,
we, the "People of the Book," were commanded no less than thirty-six times
in our Torah to love the stranger, to have empathy, to be for the most vulnerable among us, the widow, the orphan, and the outsider. Right now, so many
people are suffering from disease, from poverty, from separation.

ANWAR: Peace be with you all. We work here in America and around the
world to give a voice to folks who don't have voice. We also provide relief and
development where it's needed around the world. One of the things I'm most
proud of is the work we do with our Christian friends, our Jewish friends,
Buddhists, Hindus, and others. It is not enough for us to just do the right

thing, but to do it with others. God is happiest when we are working together. Right now, we're advocating with the US government about increasing the SNAP assistance, and working with our partners across America to get more food to people. The food pantries we support help people of all faiths. Of course, it's Ramadan now, so we're fasting. But not everyone is blessed enough to break their fast at the end of the day. We're worried about people who fast because they have to, not because they want to.

SIMONE: Food is so critical in these times, especially for our low-wage workers and those who have no regular income. Our network has done a series of engagements in rural parts of our land, and I'm a city person. I didn't know anything about rural America. But I got a call from one of the people we met in the Midwest, a dairy farmer who was absolutely in tears. She was weeping because she was having to pour out her milk because the supply chain couldn't change fast enough. That's one of the things that we've been working on in Capitol Hill—to try to provide greater flexibility in our supply chains to make sure that this dairy farmer gets her milk to market.

JONAH: We're all seeing disruption from the virus. Our congregations are having to figure out how to do funerals on Facebook, how to do prayer gatherings and Shabbat services virtually, and how to do pastoral care for one another, while at the same time supporting their health-care workers, those who have become unemployed, and those who are sheltering at home.

We are reaching out to our partners in the Catholic parishes and Muslim mosques and the mainline Protestant churches to demand that elected officials and business leaders attend to the needs of the most vulnerable. If ever there were a time for compassion and mercy and the shared interfaith sense of redemption, that time is now, and our hearts are breaking for those who are trapped in the petri dishes of suffering called jails and prisons. We're asking our people to advocate to make sure that the policies passed by Congress help those who are most needy.

An Empathy Explosion

José Andrés is a renowned chef and the founder of World Central Kitchen, an organization that provides free meals to communities hit by natural disasters.

೧~

I have been able to travel around Maryland, Virginia, Washington, New York, Queens, the Bronx, Harlem, Manhattan. What I see right and left are stories of empathy. This is an empathy explosion. People are taking care of their families and putting themselves at the service of others. In Harlem, I have seen men and women opening their restaurants, bringing back many of their employees, and even taking care of people in public housing, feeding those in desperate need. I keep going into town to bring food, and I see people who are experiencing homelessness working to protect each other, offering food to the ones they stay with under a bridge on the edge of George-town. They are proud even under these circumstances. Unfortunately, we have to have these emergencies to see some of the best moments of humanity. As we move on from this pandemic, we need to remember these moments of empathy and bring them forward to people all over the world.

Performing artist Max Auerbach awards a balcony bingo winner
with a roll of toilet paper. Munich, Germany. April 2020.

Define Our Character

Armstrong Williams is a political commentator, author, talk-show host, and media industry entrepreneur.

༌

I am the owner of a media company. We're in the content, programming, and broadcast business in network television stations across the United States. And COVID-19 is something that none of us as entrepreneurs, as private citizens, as family members, have ever seen before—the deaths, the sickness, the fear, the fact that loved ones can pass away and you can't be at their bedside to hold their hand.

My first priority has been to the hundreds of employees that we have. No way are they going to feel insecure and fear that they're going to lose their jobs. I would be willing to go into my own pockets to make sure that until we get some handle on this, my employees and my executives will have a job so they can take care of their families.

This virus is helping us determine who we are. It helps us define our character and our faith. It forces us to ask what is really important. And what's important, we found, is that we take care of our neighbors. What's most important is that we realize mankind needs mankind.

The Fear and the Panic

Courtney Meadows is a grocery clerk at Kroger in Beckley, West Virginia, and a member of the UFCW trade union.

⌒

March 13 was the day it broke loose. I was a cashier and I have never before seen the fear and the panic I did that day. You don't get social distancing in a grocery store. You don't get six feet in a grocery store. I'm very lucky that my union, the UFCW, has fought for me to be able to have PPE, to have hand sanitizers on the register, and to have relief so every thirty minutes I can go wash my hands. I have customers who come through my line and they're in a panic. I see little kids coming through my lines with masks on their face and they're scared to death. I have coworkers who are overwhelmed, and I choose more than anything to be a positive for someone—because with everything going on right now and as negative as everything seems, if I can make one person smile and I can tell them "Everything's going to be okay," and reassure them, then that's what I choose to do.

Running My School
from My Bedroom

*Dr. Dawn Brooks-DeCosta is the principal of Thurgood Marshall
Academy Lower School in Harlem, New York City.*

☙

My families are going through a lot. My teachers are feeling stressed and burnt out. Every morning we've been checking in with our students, families, and staff on their moods and how they're feeling, where they are that day and why. Then we talk about how to regulate those feelings so we can be our best selves and start the day off well. I'm trying to be compassionate, modifying my expectations, trying to support people as much as possible, and also trying to be compassionate with myself. Having three remote learners here at home with me while I'm running my school from my bedroom is not easy.

Our Children Are Watching Us

In 2013, Forbes *named Yang Lan one of the "100 Most Powerful Women in the World." She serves as chairwoman of the Sun Media Foundation in Beijing and is a Global Ambassador for the Special Olympics.*

༄

We provide art education for underprivileged children from rural areas in China. During the pandemic, we asked the children to tell their stories through paintings and drawings. More than a hundred kids between ages eight to ten sent us their work, and we assembled it into picture books with their beautiful faces on it, with and without masks. Here are some of the words they included with their drawings:

- The year of 2020 we are attacked by a terrible virus. It makes it difficult for people to breathe.
- The virus is invisible and sneaky. My town is now a battlefield.
- Mom is very nervous, reminding me constantly to wash my hands.
- We run out of masks. My dad's friend sends us the only masks that he has. We want to give him a big hug but cannot.
- Even if I just cough lightly, the whole family immediately turn to me and ask, "Are you all right?"
- There's no traffic in the city. My dad is a mechanic and his repair store has no business. I have never seen him so worried.
- My teacher texts everyone in the class in the evening to check whether we are safe.
- Every time my father goes out for grocery shopping, Mom helps him to wear double layers of masks and asks him to be careful.

- My dad volunteered to find masks for the community. He says that each one of us is like a drop of water but together we can be rivers.
- The virus is terrible but our love is more powerful.

Children's stories can give us perspective. We adults sometimes forget that our children are watching us. They are also judging us. How do the adults face a crisis? Do we treat each other with the love and care we always talk about? Do we seek solutions or are we quarreling with each other?

It's hard because we are immersed in so much information. We feel confused and are lost from time to time, and prejudices get amplified by our own fear and anger. But if we can look at this world from children's perspectives, we can see the more beautiful side of us. Through their stories and paintings, these kids are seeing kindness in ordinary people. They're showing resilience and perseverance and the determination to do better. They're discovering love. Instead of us helping them and protecting them, they are actually protecting us from being affected by negative emotions. We should learn from our children.

II.

Pain Always Leaves a Gift

INSIGHTS FOR PERSONAL CHANGE

P ain always leaves a gift," TD Jakes tells us. "There are certain things you and I wouldn't be if we'd not been hurt the way we've been hurt."

The pandemic has caused all kinds of pain—sickness, death, fear, chaos, dislocation—and no one wants to suffer. So if we're going to accept that pain leaves a gift, we have to see pain in a new light—not as an attack, or a setback, or a mistake, but as an invitation to look inside and reassess. Pain can open us up to the wisdom within.

These voices in part II invite us to see suffering as a loss of control, and to see loss of control as a spiritual opportunity. If the source of suffering is a feeling of isolation, as so many great religious traditions say, then we need a

Ayse Mehmet, whose daughter died from COVID-19, mourns with her three-year-old granddaughter. Enfield, UK. April 2020.

force that can shock us out of the conceit that we are alone, that we should be in charge, that we know what's best. Pain is that force. Pain itself is not a gift. Pain *leaves* a gift. The gift is what we see when pain opens our eyes.

We tend not to seek change when things are going well. We won't seek change even when things are going badly, unless we see the promise of a better way. These passages are about a better way. They're about cherishing the insights that come from suffering, and honoring what pain can bring to the search for truth.

Pain Always Leaves a Gift

TD Jakes is founder and senior pastor of the Potter's House, producer of the TV show The Potter's Touch, *and author of many* New York Times– *bestselling books;* Time *magazine and CNN have referred to him as "America's Best Preacher."*

❧

E verything comes as a schoolmaster to teach a lesson, to bring correction and redirection. And I think COVID-19—maybe it should have been called Correction-19—has brought some correction to our understanding of ourselves.

We have become too tribal. We've divided into too many segments: millennials, boomers, Blacks, Whites, Browns, Democrats, Republicans, us and them, not just nationally, but globally. This pandemic is making us rethink what humanity is.

There are so many lessons to be learned here. At the time when Christians celebrate the Resurrection of Christ, and the Jews celebrate Passover, and the Muslims prepare to observe the month of Ramadan, this pandemic came and brought suffering. God has never hidden from us that suffering is part of the journey. It is the dignity that we bring to the suffering that determines the outcome.

I woke up a couple of weeks ago, and I was crying and I couldn't quit. It took me about two or three hours to stop crying because I felt so bad for so many people. Maybe I had taken one call too many, or listened to one child scream too loud, or one daughter crying over not being able to touch her mother.

Funerals in our culture are a big thing. For Black people, sometimes it's the only time you get to be important. And I grieved for all of those people who never got to be memorialized, their families never got to have closure.

I grieved for all those bodies in all of those trailers, stacked up in a way that I thought I would never see in my lifetime. And I recognized the sum total of the weight of that pain on those families, and I just started crying for them. And I don't run from that kind of pain. I run *into* it, because that is that kind of pain that makes us human.

It takes strength to hang in there when everything inside us wants to get away. But pain always leaves a gift. Look for it. It will be a morsel of wisdom, a deeper strength, a greater tenacity, a new perspective. Pain always leaves a gift, even if it's left in a wheelchair, even if it's left in a hospital bed. Through every abuse or misuse, there are certain things that you and I would not be if we had not been hurt the way we have been hurt.

And we receive the gifts from the pain of the people who went before us. The cures we have now come through the suffering of people who succumbed to that disease so we could find a cure. What we need to do is make sure that all of those who died didn't die for nothing, that we learned something, that we justify their lives by discovering something that protects the next generations. We want to be better coming out than we were going in.

Already a lot of good things are happening in the midst of the bad things. America is rethinking itself. It's reshaping itself. It's honoring people that it ignored. We're looking at the disparities that exist in the African-American and the Latino communities with honesty without people saying, "You are race-baiting." We have lost our deafness in this moment and we can hear.

How We Squander Our Hours of Pain

Marianne Williamson is an author, spiritual thought leader, and political activist.

There is so much grief in our country right now. But our grief is not just a mental-health issue that individuals are dealing with. Our pain emerges from a larger mental-health issue than just our own: how lovelessly we've been organizing human civilization for decades, and where that lovelessness has taken us. We were created to love one another, and the fact that we have collectively proceeded to organize our society in a way so blatantly counter to that purpose is threatening to destroy us.

How can we speak of unity when our political and economic systems systematically separate us? When a gap between right and left, rich and poor, are at the core of our functioning, how can we speak of unity in any meaningful way without a willingness to challenge those systems? To speak of unity, true unity, is by definition to challenge the most fundamental economic and political precepts on which we have come to rely. In a world where so much is based on procuring for the rich at the expense of the poor, there is too little unity because there is too little love.

That's why love is so radical. It puts humanitarian concerns before economic principles, and our love for each other before our ability to exploit each other. And any talk of unity that fails to address those things is but a "resounding gong and a clanging cymbal."

There are far more people who love than do not love, but our love for one another must be more than a feeling. It must be put into action. In order to love in a way that overrides the forces of disunity, we must love with as much conviction as that with which some people hate. Easy love will not do the job. Convenient love will not do the job. Only a fierce love, a brutally honest love, a love that is willing to look squarely into the face of a political and economic system that refuses to love, will be powerful enough to change the world.

A serious love takes courage—the courage of radical truth-telling and a willingness to go against the grain of what is accepted as permissible in a society addicted to pleasing oneself and others. If we want to re-create the world, we are going to have to stand for love in places where it's often unpopular. A loveless world order will not give up its power easily.

Something very good can come from this period of our collective grief, but only if we're willing to learn from it. Right now, we're crying, but it's good that we're crying. The earth has been crying, and we did not listen. The people of Iraq were crying, and we did not listen. Tens of millions of poor and marginalized Americans have been crying, and we did not listen. It's our turn to cry now, and hopefully these tears will transform us. We can emerge from this moment better people because of it. The poet Rilke said it magnificently: "How we squander our hours of pain." My prayer is that we do not.

Juana Gomez waits in line at a food bank.
Van Nuys, CA, USA. April 2020.

Our Nation Has an Inner Self

Alan Lightman is a novelist, theoretical physicist, and professor of humanities at MIT. Oprah Winfrey is an American talk-show host, producer, media executive, philanthropist, and author.

ᴄᴏ

OPRAH: In your book *Searching for Stars on an Island in Maine*, you wrote that you were on a boat at night on the ocean and you had a transcendent experience.

ALAN: I was coming back to an island late at night. It was after midnight. It was a clear night, and there was no one on the water. I turned off the engine and it got even quieter. Then I turned off the running lights and it got even darker, and I lay down in the boat and looked up at the sky.

OPRAH: This is just you?

ALAN: Just me. Just me on the boat, after midnight. I laid down in the boat and looked up at the sky, and I felt like I was falling into infinity. I felt like I was merging with the stars, and not only with the stars—I felt like I was merging with the cosmos. It was an incredible feeling. I felt like I was part of something larger than myself. I've been a scientist all of my life, but that experience was not reducible by the methods of science, the feeling that I had of being connected to something big.

OPRAH: I had an experience like that in 2006. I was walking along a road in Maui, in an area where the clouds had come down. We were walking through the clouds, and I could see just a sliver of a moon, and everything became so still. Just thinking about it makes my eyes water. And I felt what you were talking about, in the boat. I felt a connection between all time, all life. I just expanded. I felt like I was a part of the clouds.

ALAN: That's the same thing. And I think all of us have had experiences like this. One of the aspects of the experience that you're describing is you lose track of your body. You lose track of your ego. You lose track of yourself. You lose track of time. It's a beautiful experience.

OPRAH: You've written that we have a chance to choose a less hurried life now. We've been living too fast, we have sold our inner selves to the devil of speed, efficiency, money, hyperconnectivity, progress. You wrote a whole book on this topic called *In Praise of Wasting Time*. Do you think this is a perfect time to press reset and do what we're talking about—be more united?

ALAN: Yes. I think there might be one or two silver linings to this devastation, and one of them is that it's forcing many of us to slow down. Of course, you have to have a certain amount of privilege to be able to slow down, but I hope that we can become conscious of the frenzy of our normal lifestyle. Most of us run around checking off items on our to-do list, being connected to the grid 24/7, and we haven't had the time to think about who we are, to reflect on what's important to us, to be quiet and still. To do some introspection, which we do too little of.

OPRAH: Both the moment on the boat you described in your book and the moment that I was talking about, in Maui, both came out of stillness. So this is an opportunity to be still—I think you're onto something, doctor.

ALAN: I'm hoping that in this period we can develop a new habit of mind, a new way of being in the world, a recognition of the importance of slowing down and of stillness.

OPRAH: You say each of us has our own inner self—and of course, we know that—but you say our nation also has an inner self. I've always felt this as well. Underneath people's individual lives and decisions, there is a consciousness. Is that what you're talking about?

ALAN: Yes. I think so. For me, my inner self is the part of me that imagines, that dreams, that thinks about who I am and what's important to me. If we think about our country as a person with an inner self, then we have to ask, does it *recognize* that it has an inner self? Is it giving itself the stillness and the quiet to think about who America is and what's important to America?

OPRAH: I hope that's what we're learning to do now. You said that in rebuilding a broken world, we will have the chance to choose a less hurried life. That's what I want.

ALAN: That's what I want, too.

Stay in This Compassionate State

Naomi Campbell was one of the five original supermodels and has appeared on more than five hundred magazine covers. In 2005, she established Fashion for Relief and does extensive charity work in South Africa and across the globe. Sofonias Negussie, Rudo Gumbo, and Hope Mutua are affiliated with African Leadership University.

⌒

NAOMI: There are no borders anymore. We're all affected by the pandemic. And staying in a good mind-set and adapting to change is the best way to respond—because there is going to be a new way of life. That's just the way it is.

For me, the key to adapting is seeing the positives, and there have been a lot of positives. We're realizing now that we're dependent on others, and this dependence can trigger kindness. Each day I'm amazed by something new—like the wonderful man who had five masks, gave one to each family member, had one left, and sent it to Governor Cuomo.

People have been so creative in finding ways to stay together emotionally even when we're separated physically. One of my great joys is seeing the connection this pandemic has created among people who are all trying to make the best of our new circumstances. I'm with three young friends who are experiencing the pandemic now in Africa.

SOFONIAS NEGUSSIE: I am from Ethiopia, currently in South Africa and a member of the founding class of ALU. I agree that there are a lot of positives coming out of the pandemic. This is a strong opportunity to realize that our diversity can actually unite us. In spite of tremendous differences in the human family, we're all affected by the virus, which means there is something underneath all the differences that makes us similar—and our greatest similarity is that we need each other. That is the most positive lesson to come out of the pandemic.

RUDO GUMBO: I'm from South Africa and part of the current incoming class of ALU. I see this pandemic and the threat to our health as a call for all of us, even world leaders, to put aside everything that does not matter. It's time to realize that health is wealth and that humanity is more important than anything else. This is a beautiful invitation for us to drop what's not needed and come together and support one another.

HOPE MUTUA: I'm from Kenya, and I just graduated in the second class of the ALU. One of the things I'm particularly passionate about is women's empowerment. I think the call to unite is a call to include groups who are usually not part of the conversation. I'm especially concerned about young women and people who might not have access to the internet. How can we include them in the discussions and the solutions as we battle this pandemic and all the other problems we face?

NAOMI: I share the hope that we all can come out of this changed. As the pandemic hit, the world was going too fast, too much pollution, too much waste, too much haste. I'm grateful for the slower pace. I cherish this stillness as a chance to reflect on what I want to do differently. I want to simplify my life in so many ways. I want to do everything I can to help our world stay in this compassionate state.

Don't Stop Celebrating

Jay Shetty is an author, motivational speaker, podcast host, and former monk.

A s we try to keep our connections strong, we have to make sure we don't stop celebrating. A lot of people have had their proms pushed back, weddings postponed, anniversaries missed, vacations canceled. It's important that we stop and pause on the day we were planning a special moment and still celebrate. I saw a couple who was meant to get married, and they had pictures of all their family members in seats in the church. It was beautiful to

Friends and family celebrate Gavin Brennan's recovery from COVID-19, final chemotherapy treatment, and seventh birthday. Dedham, MA, USA. April 2020.

see. Don't stop celebrating. You can still have an incredible birthday or anniversary, an incredible moment, because the moment was about the people and about connection. It was never about the place.

When we do miss these moments, though, it will still hurt some—and there is never a need to judge or belittle anyone's pain. Honoring someone else's grief is a chance for us to grow. It's common to feel judgmental and make others feel guilty for their grief. At times, we don't want others to feel the pain *they* feel, because their pain can trigger ours. So, if we start by saying, "Let me grieve for my loss," then we can realize that the person missing a graduation may have faced as much pain as someone suffering a loss we think is much larger. Pain is something that we often think of as big or small. But that's just our perspective. We have to put ourselves in other people's shoes, and also feel the loss in our own lives. Only then can we let people heal at their own pace in their own time.

God Has Self-Limited, Says the Talmud

Rabbi Yitz Greenberg is a theologian, a scholar of Judaism, an author, and an activist.

ᴄᴏ

Here in Jerusalem, a beautiful, quiet Shabbat came to an end an hour ago. I love Sabbath days in Jerusalem. They are replenishing and spiritually nurturing. But this Sabbath was different from any that went before it.

Not one synagogue, not one church, not one mosque was open for group prayers this Shabbat in Jerusalem. All the religions agreed to use social isolation to avoid contagion.

Facing death by virus concentrates the mind religiously. With the spread of the pandemic, online searches for "prayer" skyrocketed. We all seek some religious guidance at this moment.

There are Bible sources that describe natural disasters as Divine punishment. But one of rabbinic Judaism's most important modifications of the biblical message is this: God has self-limited, says the Talmud. The biblical age of punishments and visible miracles where God openly intervenes to defeat evil forces has ended. The good news is that God has come closer so we are never alone. God shares our pain. God holds our hand. We walk together even in the valley of the shadow of death.

Yet, even as God is near and we are not alone, we have to face down our fear of death. When I love another, when I create family, when I embrace a higher cause, death and failure can inflict more pain on me by harming those I love. Our response to this increased threat must not be to give up or back away or yield to despair. Rather we should follow the Bible's overriding command to "choose life," knowing that the increased risk is worth it—for this love brings the joy that makes life worth living. In response to the pandemic of death and disease, we all need to live more deeply and well, no matter what happens to us or our loved ones—because the Bible has given us God's promise that if we choose life, then "Love is stronger than death."

A Special Responsibility
to Give Hope

Thabo Makgoba is the South African Anglican archbishop of Cape Town.

⌒

When the coronavirus struck, our economy in South Africa was already struggling. We had high unemployment with low levels of growth, and the pandemic is now destroying jobs. People's incomes are affected in unthinkable ways. But we are not alone. We may be vulnerable as a country, but so are many others. That is why this crisis is uniting all God's children in love wherever in the world they live.

We religious people have a special responsibility to give hope amidst this pandemic. When I speak about hope, it is not hope in the sense of an anesthetic to dull the throbbing pain of the current everyday reality. It is not an assurance that everyone will live happily ever after. To see hope in that way is an invitation to ultimately sink into despair and to surrender. No, hope is about acknowledging our fears, and dealing bravely with the pain, the reality, and the uncertainty brought to us by this pandemic. Only then will we have the love and the strength to turn this crisis to good.

Awakening Comes When Chaos Breaks In

Eckhart Tolle is a renowned spiritual teacher and bestselling author.

 ᐧᐧᐧ

Whenever you're experiencing any form of adversity, it's important to understand that there is a law of polarities in the world. On the one hand, you have what we could call order. When order is in your life, you are able to think positively. You are able to create. You have structure. We all want to live in an ordered universe where everything is working as it should. But we tend to forget that there is not just order in this world, there is also the other polarity, which we could call disorder, disruption, or even chaos.

No matter how careful you are, how much positive thinking you practice, at some point you will experience the other polarity. Something gets disrupted—you experience the painful breakup of a marriage or a close relationship, you lose your job, you lose your income, you lose your home, you fall ill, somebody close to you dies or suffers. All kinds of things can erupt in your life. Even people who are good at creating order will at some point experience disorder.

And disorder is necessary. Real inner growth usually does not come when things are going well. That's not where awakening happens. Awakening comes when chaos breaks into your life—when you're out of your comfort zone. You may then recognize that the most important cause of your unhappiness is not the outside world, but what you are *thinking* about the outside world, which is the mental narrative. Your state of consciousness is always primary. All else is secondary.

Disorder gives you an opportunity to become aware of what your mind is doing. Is your unhappiness actually produced by the situation that you're in, or is the greater part of your unhappiness produced by a narrative in your mind that refuses to accept the present moment?

Sometimes people don't understand what real acceptance is. They think, "Okay, I need to accept that my life has completely fallen apart. There is nothing I can do, and I need to accept it." No. All you need to accept is this moment. Accepting the moment doesn't mean that you cannot take action. In fact, more intelligent action arises out of acceptance of the present moment than out of rejection of the present moment.

Accepting the present moment means accepting uncertainty. During the pandemic, a huge amount of uncertainty has come into people's lives, which means you don't know what is going to happen. Before, you *thought* you knew what was going to happen. Ultimately, that was an illusion, too. But at least things seemed to be relatively ordered.

Now thoughts of uncertainty are creating a lot of worry. When you worry, you are creating a narrative in your mind about a future that is worse than what you have now—and the emotion you're experiencing reflects the narrative your mind is creating, but it's not the reality of what is going on now.

Spiritual practice is important for seeing the reality—for being able to observe this thing in your life that we could call uncertainty and, instead of rejecting it, coming to terms with it. This gives you a chance for a shift in consciousness. And if enough people experience this shift, the collective changes, and then the world changes—because the human-made world is a product of collective consciousness.

One of my favorite parables is in the New Testament, where Jesus talks about a man who built his house on the sand, and the winds came, and the floods came, and the house was swept away. Then there is a man who digs

deep until he finds the rock and he built his house on the rock. And the winds
came, and the floods came, and the house was not swept away—because it
was built on the rock.

What we need to do is dig deep and find the rock, which means the foundation, the being of yourself, so that you are rooted in the being. And then
when the winds come, as they are coming now, the floods come, and the
winds beat against the house, your house will stand. The storm doesn't devas-
tate you. You are not threatened anymore. To some extent, your state of consciousness is no longer dependent on the outside world—because you have
found the rock, which is the being.

When you find the being, you find love, because love is recognizing "the
other" as yourself—recognizing that the being of the other is the being of you,
also—the one consciousness expressing itself, disguising itself, in many, many
forms.

This Is an Apocalypse

*Richard Rohr is a Franciscan friar, a globally recognized religious
teacher, a* New York Times*–bestselling author, and the founder of the
Center for Action and Contemplation in Albuquerque, New Mexico.*

თ

The great spiritual traditions have much to teach us about this moment.
I'll contribute my little bit in a way I know is unusual for a Catholic—
I'll bring a little Scripture to this question.

There are two forms of biblical literature that are almost always confused.

The Cathedral Church of St. John the Divine is converted into a field hospital. New York, NY, USA. April 2020.

One is called prophetic and one is called apocalyptic. I want to describe what we mean by the apocalyptic and why what we're going through right now is an apocalyptic event.

What apocalyptic means, you've been told, I'm sure, is to pull back the veil, to reveal the underbelly of reality. It uses hyperbolic images, stars falling from the sky, the moon turning to blood. The closest thing would be contemporary science fiction, where suddenly you're placed in an utterly different world, where what you used to call "normal" doesn't apply anymore. That perfectly describes this event, perhaps more than anything else in our lifetime. Even the two world wars were largely associated with the Northern Hemisphere. But this truly is global.

So hear this word rightly—it is *meant* to shock: this is an *apocalypse*, happening to us in our lifetime, that's leaving us utterly out of control. We're grasping to retake control, and I hope we can. But I think we're all reminded that we can't take control totally.

Now, there's a giveaway in all of the three apocalyptic sections of the three Synoptic Gospels. In Matthew 24, hidden there in the middle of the stars falling from the sky, it says, "All this is only the beginning of the birth pangs." That's very telling. The beginning of the birth pangs. We hear it as threat. Anything that upsets our normalcy is threat. But you can see it isn't. In Luke 21, he puts right in the middle: "Your endurance will win you your souls." Again, such a telling line. In Mark 13, he says, "Stay awake" four times in the last paragraph. In other words, "Learn the lesson that this has to teach you." It points to everything that we take for granted and says, "don't take anything for granted." That is an apocalyptic event. It reframes reality in a radical way.

We would have done history a great favor if we would have understood apocalyptic literature. It's not *threat*. It's not the end of the world. Listen closely: It's the end of *worlds*—our *worlds that we have created*. We're not trying to literally describe the end of the world. We're trying to describe what it feels like when everything falls apart. It's not a threat. It's an invitation to depth. It's what it takes to wake people up to the real, to the lasting, to what matters.

Even before this happened, we were talking at the Center about predoom spirituality. That's the word we were using to look at the state of the planet, the state of our politics, the state of human relations. It looked like we were on the edge of collapse. And then *this* happened, this pandemic. Nothing softer than "apocalyptic event" is appropriate. But it's only for those who are ready to hear and to see it.

Our best response is to end our fight with reality, stop pushing it away. We benefit from anything that approaches a welcoming prayer—diving into the change positively, preemptively, saying, "Come, reality; teach me your good lessons." That's the practice we need, to lessen our resistance, our tight grabbing of things. And that doesn't mean we don't work for good. We're all excited about the possibility of a vaccine. But before we can get there, we have to offer reality a deep "Yes." Only then can its lessons come through. We practice silence, but I am with any school that emphasizes surrender.

You Who Have Fallen

Peter Gabriel is a singer-songwriter, record producer, and humanitarian activist.

⌒

I'm in London and in lockdown. I've been asked for a few reflections on what's going on, and I wrote some words which may become a song. I'm calling it "Who Wears the Crown?"

Stars up above us on this empty London street.
A springtime's full of life alive, the air so soft and sweet.
The world is turning once again, and when the wheel will stop,
The world will form as something else and then the coin will drop.

And out come all the questions, the questions we don't ask,
As we close in from a distance and stay protected by the mask.
For all of you who have fallen, no more is it your task.
We'll make sure that light's infectious, that's still glowing in your
    cask.

What Gets Revealed
Must Get Healed

Chad Veach is the lead pastor of Zoe Church, a youth-oriented parish in Los Angeles, California.

༄

Times of crisis don't build character; they *reveal* character. That's what I love about this time—it's revealing things inside of us. Maybe it's revealed compassion in your heart. Maybe it's caused outbursts of anger. That's okay. What gets revealed must get healed. And sometimes it takes a crisis to reveal it. Sometimes it takes us getting pressed, our backs pushed up against the wall, for us to find out what's inside. It's rare that we're on the mountaintop of success and we cry out for help. It's usually when we're in the valley of despair. This crisis has brought us to that place of need. We're not just dependent upon a stimulus check. We're dependent upon the good of humanity.

We're depending on others to say of us, "Their problem is my problem." And others are depending on us to say the same of them. We've got to be connected. The worst thing that any of us could do right now is live on isolation island. Have you ever been there? Isolation island is when you go and you pout, "Nobody likes me, everybody hates me." But you can't live on isolation island. You've got to come back into the community because when you're connected, it means you're committed. And it's through our commitment to each other that we see the good.

This is a call to unity. What's the opposite of unity? It's di-vision. Literally two different visions. So this is a call to lay aside our different visions and

Men pray at a ceremony commemorating the 115th anniversary of Juneteenth. Minneapolis, MN, USA. June 2020.

come together for the good of humanity. What we need right now are people who are willing to get uncomfortable. We need people who are willing to say, "I'm answering the call, and I'm going to do my part to bring us together."

The Call on the Inside

DeVon Franklin is an award-winning film and TV producer, New York Times*–bestselling author, speaker, and spiritual coach.*

⌒

When you get a call on your phone that you're not ready to answer, you can send it to voice mail. You can delay it or deny it. But that's not the kind of call I'm concerned with. It's not a real calling. A real calling is this: a strong inner impulse toward action accompanied by a conviction from God.

This means that the calling on our life comes from the inside, not from the outside. To answer the call on your life, you have to listen from the inside. But we have trouble hearing the call from the inside because we're just too distracted. We have the news running 24/7, our phones beeping all day, we are checking Instagram, Twitter, Facebook, texts, emails. What we have not checked is the message in our spirit that God has deposited.

Why don't we have the power we want? Why don't we have the peace we want? Why aren't we as productive as we want? It's not because God is not good, it's because we are not taking the time to listen. When was the last time you took a moment to get silent so that you could hear the call on the inside of your spirit? I believe each one of us has a calling to unite like never before, if we would just take the time to listen.

What does it mean to unite? Unite means to be made as one. You take many things that don't seem like they fit and you make them as one.

Each of us has a calling in our spirit to unite as one. Some of you may feel like you're a superhero fighting a losing battle—but that's because you're going at it by yourself. You've got to connect with other heroes. This call to unite is for all of us. We have to unite like never before because there are evils in the world that only unity can defeat.

The Suffering Ends

Tony Robbins is an American author, business strategist, life coach, speaker, and philanthropist. He has been married to Sage Robbins for over twenty years.

༚

SAGE: What's really moved me during the pandemic is the beauty of human beings giving their gifts. That's our nature, giving and serving from a generous spirit. Unfortunately, sometimes that spirit gets diminished out of unconscious expectations that we have to get something back in return. To counter that, we need to ask the question, "How can I serve?"

TONY: The challenge is fear. If you're a human, you're facing fear right now, and fear separates us. It's an old problem. We have a two-million-year-old brain, a survival brain, and it's always asking, "What do I do to avoid pain? How do I fight or flight or freeze so I don't get hurt?" And that leads us to separation. We separate from ourselves, from our partners, from our friends, from our companies, from our creator. And the moment we do that, we suffer. Separation equals suffering.

The secret is for us to see that there are two options: suffer or grow. And I think most of us don't want to suffer anymore. I think we've suffered enough. It's time for us to grow. Growth requires us to get outside ourselves, and we get outside of ourselves by serving others. So, as Sage said, we have to ask ourselves, "How can we serve? What can I give? How can I help or contribute?" There are people who are suffering more than you are, no matter how tough you may have it. And the gift of humanity, what makes us a human family, is the spiritual side of us that says, "If I can just focus on helping someone else, if I can get out of my own head and into my heart, the suffering ends.

Never Waste a Hurt

Rick Warren, often called "America's Pastor," is the founder of Saddleback Church in Lake Forest, California, and bestselling author of The Purpose Driven Life. *He has led response teams in thirty-four national and international pandemics and disasters, and prayed at two presidential inaugurations.*

಄

These days are a time of great stress, but they are also a time for great learning, and *if* we learn the right lessons, we'll all benefit from this ordeal. We should never waste a hurt. Let me suggest two positive things we've learned, and two areas that we've learned we need to work on.

First, we've seen that good people will sacrifice for the common good in tough times. People respond with their best when the best is asked of them. We often assume that people can't change, or won't change, or that they'll never change, so all we can do is just accept that reality. But this pandemic has proven that false. People *can and will* make huge, radical behavioral changes for good when they're motivated by seeing a clear benefit. This learning should give leaders hope.

Second, we've seen that many are learning to appreciate the people in service industries who serve them in ways that they previously ignored. The term *essential workers* used to mean high-paying jobs, but now we realize how *essential* grocery truckers are, and hospital janitors, and health-care workers, and school teachers. *These* are the people we can't do without. There's a new awareness and a new appreciation. That's a good thing.

But third, in this pandemic we've witnessed the enormous economic disparity in our nation. This inequity is a surprise for many. They've never noticed. People have said "We're all in the same boat," but actually we are not. Right now, we're all in the same *storm*, but everyone is riding out the storm in different ways. Some fortunate people are in a yacht, working at home with high-speed internet, while others are in a rowboat without a paddle and out of work. Then the homeless are just hanging on to a piece of driftwood. How do you "shelter at home" when you don't have a home?

Fourth, we're learning that the pandemic created two different kinds of tension: one is physical, and the other is emotional and spiritual. Medical professionals are battling the DISEASE of the virus. But others of us are helping people cope with the *DIS-EASE* of the pandemic—the resulting stress, anxiety, loneliness, and depression created by quarantining, social distancing, and the closing of businesses, schools, churches, concerts, and in-person sporting events. As a pastor counseling a congregation of over thirty thousand people, I know firsthand that people are struggling emotionally from the changes they've had to adapt to. The longer this pandemic continues, the greater the damage it does to lives and relationships.

COVID-19 is devastating millions of people who will never get sick from the virus, but they've lost a lot this year—lost celebrations, lost graduations, lost opportunities, lost jobs. Think how many weddings, funerals, and baby showers had to be downsized or canceled. How many relatives missed an important moment because they couldn't travel? Long after a vaccine or cure is discovered, there will be a tsunami of grief around the world as people realize what they missed or lost. The spiritual cost of a global pandemic can't be ignored. That's why, even though our church has not resumed public worship services, I've never been busier. We're feeding hundreds of thousands of families and helping people online learn the lessons and habits that will sustain them through these days.

Here's a habit I encourage you to learn in this pandemic: *Start and end your day refueling your soul.* Every human being has a limited amount of emotional, spiritual, and physical energy for each day. Some people entered this pandemic year with their emotional and spiritual tanks full. Others began the pandemic with a half-empty tank. But some people were already depleted—their tank was empty even before the pandemic hit. These are the people I'm most concerned about.

The good news is that there are some simple and practical ways you can get your tank refilled. You know, Christians, Muslims, and Jews all accept the Book of Psalms as the word of God, and Psalm 23 says, *"He [God] restores my soul!"* So let me suggest a simple habit that you follow every day during this pandemic: Get a Bible in a modern translation like the *New Living Translation* (NLT), open it up to the book of Psalms (in the very middle of the Bible), and leave it open by your bedside. Then, when you wake up in the morning, sit on the side of your bed and read some from Psalms before you do anything else. Don't look at your phone first! Don't look at the news! *Refuel your soul.* Read until you hit a thought that speaks to you, then stop. It doesn't matter *how long* you read. Just read until something speaks to you, then stop. Make spiritual and emotional refueling the first act of your day. Then leave your Bible open to where you stopped. At the end of your day, the last thing you do before you go sleep is to pick up where you ended that morning. Start reading again until something speaks to you again. It can be comforting or challenging—*both* will refuel your soul. The timeless insights that have sustained billions of people through wars and plagues and suffering for thousands of years are all right there in the Bible.

Another habit that will help you through this pandemic is this: *Show grace to yourself and to others.* You need to treat yourself the way God treats you! Be kind to yourself. Realize that every day that this crisis continues, it's drawing down your reserves, and everyone else's, too. You're being drained daily, just like a punctured tire goes flat. Don't expect to work at the same level of efficiency and effectiveness you had before this crisis. If you find yourself exhausted only a couple hours after you got up—you're normal. Be gentle with yourself . . . and with others, too—because everybody's having a tough time. Show yourself the same grace that God shows you. And know this: You matter to God, you matter to me, and you matter to a lot of people that you don't even realize. If you're feeling hopeless and maybe have even thought about taking your life, please don't. Please don't. We need you alive! If you're hurting right now, or grieving a loss, or feeling anxious or lonely, email me: PastorRick@saddleback.com. My team and I can help you.

Lanee Jackson participates in an Essential Not Expendable rally in Washington, DC, USA. April 2020.

What Schools Should Have Been Teaching All Along

Esther Wojcicki is a journalist and educator and author of How to Raise Successful People.

෮෮

All across the world right now, families are struggling with homeschooling. In the short term, it's stressful, but I think this is also a huge opportunity to change the way we've been teaching for the last five hundred years.

Parents and teachers need to learn to trust the child to play an important role in her or his own education—with a focus on self-learning and the priority of building community. This is what schools should have been teaching all along, and now the needs and the new circumstances of the pandemic give us an opportunity to act on it.

I started a blog to help parents with this approach—focusing on building a sense of community and not so much about the homework that the kids might not have been able to do. Parents are getting so upset over the homework. Does it really matter?

I teach English and journalism at Palo Alto High School, and my students decided that instead of fundraising for the student newspaper, they would fundraise for people who didn't have food. Empowering students to build a sense of community turns them loose as self-learners. My students poured all their energy into identifying a charity, raising money for Second Harvest, and collecting a thousand dollars in just three days. It gives me chills thinking about how empathetic they became. And it spread. The students got excited, they talked to their friends about it, and the whole neighborhood started to feel more like a community.

An emphasis on compassion and on self-learning is going to cause anxiety at first, because it's different. But it's also essential if students are going to grow up and do the things they're hoping to do in life. And that's the goal of education, after all—creating a person who feels empowered to follow their dreams.

In the Soul of the Parent

Dr. Shefali Tsabary is a clinical psychologist, family therapist, wisdom teacher, and author. Maria Shriver is a journalist, author, former First Lady of California, and founder of the Women's Alzheimer's Movement.

⌒

MARIA: Is this a moment to birth something new?

SHEFALI: Absolutely. Parents have an opportunity to connect with their children in a way that they have never had the time, energy, or space to do before.

MARIA: But if you are a parent who is stressed out about home schooling, wondering if school is ever going to start again, it may not feel like an opportunity. What's your best advice to that parent and child?

Trisha Vix places a crown on her daughter, Patrice Toussaint,
whose senior prom was canceled due to the pandemic.
Brooklyn, NY, USA. May 2020.

SHEFALI: Before the pandemic, one out of every three children in the US suffered from an anxiety disorder. This is an opportunity to turn that around. We have been fast-tracking children on this endless conveyor belt toward a false utopia of happiness and success, and it's failed. Children are not feeling successful. They're not feeling happy. They're feeling angst ridden. They are stressed out with record levels of anxiety, suicidality, and disconnection. The pandemic has offered us a turning point, but the way we turn depends on the consciousness of the parent. Can the parent use this moment to see how they were pushing their children toward this stress-driven life?

MARIA: How do you make that turn, regardless of the age of your children?

SHEFALI: We turn by looking at ourselves in the mirror and admitting that the way we were parenting wasn't working. If you have that conversation, your children will tell you that pushing them to strive on this linear path toward success is toxic for them. So first we have to listen. We have to connect with our children through different ideals. It is not about an overdriven, stressed-out existence; it is about asking them how they want to live their lives.

MARIA: Do you envision parents and children of all ages gathering around kitchen tables, speaking honestly, saying, "I got it wrong. I wanted things for you without even asking what you wanted—and now I want to change course and hear what you want"?

SHEFALI: I don't hold any utopian ideas around happy conversations, but I think we need to ask our children and ourselves, "What was working?" And be honest about all the things we were too attached to—our wealth, our status, our need for validation from the outside world.

This is the great pause. We've been speeding along the path of the ego, driven toward false ideals of success and achievement. Now we need to shed those false ideals and begin to live authentically. Our children need us to focus on things that matter to their well-being, not to our ego. It isn't about our ego anymore, because now we realize that we don't know the future, and we can't predict their lives. All we have is the present moment, and we have to tune in to our children's authentic selves in this moment.

MARIA: How do we do that? What are the qualities of a conscious parent?

SHEFALI: The parent has to see that they are projecting the unmet needs and fantasies of their broken self onto their children.

MARIA: Repeat that! Repeat that! Repeat that!

SHEFALI: The parent needs to be aware that they are looking for completion through their children. This is the number-one mistake we make.

And actually it is not a mistake; it is a colossal unconsciousness that we pass on to our children generation after generation. This moment gives us the opportunity to disrupt that unconscious slumber, that zombified existence where we're robotically passing on our emotional baggage.

So the first step is that parents need to be aware of what they're doing. The second step is that they choose to heal themselves so their children are unburdened and can live out their own destiny.

MARIA: You've also said that to be a conscious parent you have to be honest with yourself about what you didn't get, and what you're still longing for. And then talk with your child about mistakes you've made, unmet needs you've had, and how you want to show up differently. Is this right?

SHEFALI: Yes. For me, the pivotal unification is inner unification. Most of us live in a false self, pleasing others, looking for validation from the outside. Most of us were robbed of our true self—that's why the healing has to occur within. Everything births in the soul of the parent, so if you want your children's future to be resplendent with beauty and luminosity, it has to occur in your consciousness first.

A Chance to Start Anew

Eva Longoria is an actress, producer, director, activist, and businesswoman.

༄

We have a chance to start anew and come out kinder—and all around us we're seeing signs that it's happening. Workers are putting their families at risk so they can take care of ours, chefs are pivoting from their restaurants to focus on feeding the homeless, therapists are donating their time online to those who need help, perfume companies are making hand sanitizers instead of fragrances, people are using their skill in sewing to make masks for first responders.

Everyone has something to give, and they're giving it. When we're seeing acts of kindness we've never seen before, when we're navigating challenges we've never faced before, when we're responding to others' fears even when they're not *our* fears, we're seeing the proof that we can have a better world. In these moments, we *are* a better world. When we emerge from this pandemic, we have to remember that our kindness is not just for crises and special occasions, it's what we owe ourselves and each other, always.

When Others Are Kind

Dr. Daniel Fessler is a professor of biological anthropology specializing in evolutionary medicine at the University of California, Los Angeles.

ᢙ

O ur species is remarkable in its cooperativeness. We are unlike any other species on the planet in that way. But we aren't helpful toward everyone all the time. We decide whether to be helpful toward others as a function of how they are acting themselves. Our human nature leads us to be kind when others are kind. We experience a positive emotion—scientists call it *elevation*—when we witness other people being kind toward strangers.

This uplifting experience is associated with hormonal changes in the body. We experience a reduction of stress when we see other people being positive toward one another. And the opposite is true when we see people acting in a self-interested fashion. We are motivated to respond in the way that we see others acting around us. You can think of kindness as being contagious. When we see people helping others where there is nothing in it for them, we are motivated to do the same. That actually changes our emotional and personal experience, and our physiology as well.

But there is an exception. My research team has shown that the way we respond to seeing other people being kind depends on what our expectations are. When people who expect others to be cooperative and altruistic see those positive actions, they experience an uplifting emotion. But when people are more cynical and they expect other people to be selfish, they can see the same event and not experience anything positive at all. Now where do those negative expectations come from? They come from past experience. So when we act with kindness, and a cynical person who is expecting something negative

A woman makes a heart shape with her hands in support
of health-care workers. Malaga, Spain. May 2020.

instead sees something positive, we're changing their expectations, and thus their experience. We can get a positive feedback loop going, an upward spiral where everyone is becoming more uplifted and more altruistic in turn.

How we act toward each other shapes the community we live in, the society we live in, and ultimately the planet we inhabit. Each of us can begin with a small act, just a smile or nod toward a stranger, to shape each other's experience and make the world a kinder and more cooperative place.

I Thought the Prophets Were Gone

Barbara Holmes is a spiritual teacher, activist, and scholar focused on African American spirituality. She is president emerita of United Theological Seminary of the Twin Cities, and author of Joy Unspeakable: Contemplative Practices of the Black Church.

⌒

I want to unite around a word of hope. And I need a pretty strong word of hope because, for most of us, anxiety has been running rampant. We need something strong. We need something to stand on. And for this word of hope, I am taking a lyric from Pulitzer Prize–winning hip hop artist Kendrick Lamar and my grandmother, who, amazingly enough, said the same thing at different times: "We Gon' Be Alright." We may not be the same, but we're going to be all right.

How do we know we're going to be all right? We know this because centuries have gone by, ancestors have gone through the same things we're going through, and we have survived. And we've seen that people who survive, survive well together. So, everything is going to be all right because we know what to do. We know what's working. We know what's not working. We know we're being given an opportunity to revise, change, and rethink everything. We're being given a chance to unite.

United, we can satisfy the needs of the poor throughout the globe. United, we can develop new health-care systems that pay attention to local needs as well as corporate goals. United, we can form a community that transcends borders, that transcends our differences, that transcends our desire to be radically individual. In the end, we're being called to joy.

I've written a lot about joy. And one of the things that I'm certain of is that joy and happiness are not the same thing. Happiness tends to be tied to your finances, to your success, to your education, and joy is something that's cosmically seated in the center of your soul. It's something that you feel. It's something that you inherit. You find joy even in the midst of grief. There is always joy to be found. The problem is that this joy that we are seeking may not come until a few tears are shed. But united we can overcome anything, and begin to create a new world.

In seeking a new world, I look to the prophets a lot, and I was jokingly telling a friend that I thought the prophets were gone because they're no longer available for speaking engagements. But I failed to recognize that they're here; they just don't look the same. They're in torn jeans. They're rhyming and rapping. But they're leading the way, seeking a new world—and while it is coming, I urge you to bless someone, to forgive someone who doesn't deserve it, and be ready to join hands in joy, because we're all going to be all right. We're not going to be the same. But we're all going to be all right.

We Have Paused, Now We Must Reset

Sir Ken Robinson was a globally celebrated author, speaker, and education and innovation expert. In 1998, he led the British government's advisory committee on creative and cultural education—and was knighted in 2003 for his efforts. His 2009 TED Talk, "Schools Kill Creativity," remains the most viewed TED Talk of all time, and he has been called "one of the world's elite thinkers on creativity and innovation." Sir Ken died on August 21, 2020, after a short battle with cancer. His contribution to The Call to Unite, captured below, was his final public address to humanity during his lifetime.

✺

Like everybody else we are in lockdown, in our case in London, with many of us trying to look ahead to a time when we might get back to normal. The question is, what type of normal do we want to get back to? Is it the normal we have left behind us? I think it shouldn't be.

I've long felt that we are facing two major climate crises. There is a climate crisis enveloping all of us; it was with us before the pandemic hit, and it's still there waiting to be dealt with. But there has also been a long-term crisis in our way of life, in the lack of fulfillment many people feel, in the tensions, stresses, and anxieties we face. All of this is related to our neglect of our relationship with the natural world, with the other creatures we share this planet with, and with the ecosystems we depend upon.

There is a connection between our relationship with the natural world and the way we have come to think about education. Let me put it this way: most mass systems of education came into being in the eighteenth century, and they are mostly based on the process of industrialism. The Industrial Revolution brought about massive changes in manufacturing, in technology, and it created the modern world we now live in.

Part of the Industrial Revolution ran through agriculture, and made dramatic differences in the way we farm. Industrial farming has been focused primarily on output—more, bigger, better—with the focus being on the plant. That may seem obvious, but the result of it has been that topsoil has been eroded and degraded all around the planet. We all depend on this thin smear of soil for everything that grows.

The thing is, there are alternatives to these industrial systems, which are variously called organic or sustainable farming. In these alternative systems, the emphasis is on diversity, on crops being grown in close proximity so they create their own natural protection. They create conditions where the insects and wildlife that depend upon them flourish. In sustainable versions of farming the emphasis is not on the plant; it's on the soil.

Sustainable farmers know we have to get the soil right. If we get the soil right, then life will flourish indefinitely. This is not the case when chemicals are killing all of the nutrients upon which life ultimately depends. We have had great short-term success with these industrial systems, but they have led to a catastrophic price. We have to make a new settlement with the earth by thinking differently about our relationship with it.

Now, we have replicated the mistakes we've made in industrial farming in our social systems, and particularly in education. Our education systems are also based on output, on yield. We put our children through these systems year after year, age group by age group, and the emphasis has been on output, on test data, on scores, on graduation rates, on everybody going to college and getting a degree. This is as pointless and unsustainable in its own way as are agriculture systems based on industrial principles.

A teacher and her students participate in an outdoor learning demonstration. Brooklyn, NY, USA. September 2020

Human beings are like the rest of life on earth. We flourish under certain conditions and we wither in others.

The other parallel is this: just as sustainable agricultural systems are based on cultivating the soil, our communities, cities, neighborhoods, and schools flourish when the culture is right.

Great teachers, great principals, and great school systems understand that you don't make a successful education system based on driving people through pointless systems of tests, output, and data-driven hurdles. They understand that the way you get people to flourish is by recognizing their individuality, the great diversity in the depth of people's talents, and by creating a mixed culture in schools that values the sciences, the arts, technology, and the driving force of individual passions.

In other words, successful schools don't focus on output, they focus on culture—in the same way that sustainable farmers focus on the soil. If you get the culture right, everything else takes care of itself, and that really means a culture of compassion, of collaboration, of empathy, and of valuing individuals and our social lives through joint participation.

If we have found out anything in this pandemic, it's how fundamentally we rely on these sorts of processes when the chips are down. So, I believe profoundly that getting back to normal won't work.

We have pressed pause on many of our social systems. It's time to press reset on them as well.

The pandemic has created a huge shift for schools—for families, for children, and for educators all around the world. It's the first time in hundreds of years that whole education systems have been turned off. The treadmill has stopped.

Children have been at home with their parents, with their relatives, trying to come to terms with how to carry on learning in this new situation. The most successful examples of this have been when parents haven't felt the need to replicate school. There is a big difference in learning and school. Learning is the most natural process in the world. We love to learn. We are deeply curious creatures, highly creative, deeply compassionate, and highly collaborative. We love to learn from a very early age. But not everyone gets on with education, and a lot of people don't like school. The problem is not teachers, or kids, or families; it's how we do school. We've come to think of schools as places that resemble standardization and factory life. There is no reason for schools to be that way. We can reinvent school. We can revitalize learning and reignite the creative compassion of our communities if we think differently when we try to go back to normal.

How do we do all of that?

There is a big parallel between what needs to happen in education and in the environmental movement. It's based on the same principles, and it's achieving the same ends. We need to see that real social change comes from the ground up, through people cultivating the grass roots. It's a mistake to believe that we need to wait until some enlightened politician comes along and shows us the way. That happens from time to time, but more often than not, it doesn't. The real power is with the people. It's getting people to share ideas, to collaborate, to work together to see future possibilities, and to bring them about through joint projects and through the support that comes from compassionate collaboration.

We don't live in the world as other creatures do. We create ideas about the world. We create, in a word, cultures, and our cultures define us in more ways than we can really see or suspect. The world is full of diverse cultures, but we have a common set of fortunes to confront. We are a single species, with other species, on one planet. We need to reimagine what that could look like—and create a new sort of world and a new kind of normal.

III.

Magic Enters the Room

STORIES AND PRACTICES OF
TRANSFORMATION

I just laid on my bunk and I began to think of everything in my life that went wrong, everything I had done that I wasn't proud of, everyone I had hurt. Then I decided to do the one thing that I could still do in my small cell."

Those are the words of Lawrence Bartley, telling the story of his spiritual transformation halfway through his twenty-seven-year stay in prison. Lawrence and other teachers in part III share the exercises they've turned to in times of grief and regret, and the practices they've used to help themselves grow.

We hear the voices of a Hindu monk translating Sanskrit verses, a Christian minister who is a teacher of Zen, and a music legend who shares the spiritual practices she taught herself as a homeless teen. Brian McLaren tells

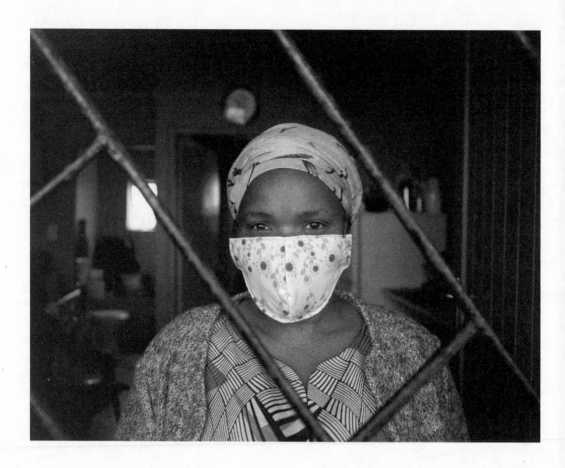

Alphonia Zali looks out from her apartment.
Cape Town, South Africa. May 2020.

us about the time he arrived home from cancer treatments for his six-year-old son, and suddenly felt that we are all suffering the same grief, and we are all held in the same love.

Each exercise and experience described—from the practical to the mystical—has the same theme and the same aim: ending isolation. Amidst the many approaches, Brie Stoner offers context: Any practice that helps us release our stories and relax into a state of trust is a positive practice, she says. And there is a deep connection between inner change and outer change. When we're doing our inner work, we're not just doing it for ourselves; we're doing it for the sake of the whole.

Changing the world is an inside job.

I Saw the Cause of All Suffering

Byron Katie is an author, speaker, and founder of The Work, a method of psychological/spiritual inquiry.

∽

One day, after more than a decade of suicidal despair, as I lay sleeping on the floor (I believed that I didn't deserve a bed), a cockroach crawled over my foot. I opened my eyes, and all my depression and rage, all the thoughts that had been tormenting me—all thoughts, period—were gone. I saw the cause of all suffering. I saw that my depression had nothing to do with the world around me. It was caused by what I believed about the world. I realized that when I believed my thoughts, I suffered, but when I didn't believe them, I didn't suffer, and that this is true for every human being. Freedom is as simple as that. I was intoxicated with joy. I felt that if my joy were told, it would blow the roof off the house—off the whole planet. I still feel that way.

Our unexamined thoughts that argue with reality create all the suffering in our lives. There has never been a stressful feeling that wasn't caused by attaching to an untrue thought. We can't let go of those thoughts, no matter how hard we try. But if we question them, they let go of us. That is the way out.

Don't believe me. Try it for yourself. When your next stressful thought comes, either you'll believe it or you'll question it. There's no other option. Let's question it. What is running through your head now? Maybe it's that your mother might get the coronavirus. You might lose your job. Maybe you're judging your husband or wife or your employee or your boss, judging the politicians, judging God. Identify the thought that is frightening you or making you miserable, and let's examine it with four questions. Write the thoughts down on a Judge-Your-Neighbor Worksheet (you can download one free at www.thework.com).

1. *Is it true?*

> Take your time. The Work is meditation. Give a one-syllable answer—yes or no, without any explanation or justification. If your answer is no, go to question three. If it's yes,

2. *Can you absolutely know that it's true?*

> Never mind what people say. Let your answer come from inside.

3. *How do you react, what happens, when you believe that thought?*

> Get in touch with your emotions. Identify the effects of believing that thought. Be detailed and specific.

4. *Who would you be without that thought?*
    Imagine yourself without your story. What do you see now when you look at the person you judged? How does it feel?

Now turn that thought around. If you wrote, "The coronavirus is ruining my life," turn it around to "The coronavirus isn't ruining my life" and notice the ways the opposite is just as true as—or maybe even truer than —your original thought. "I'm finding more time for myself. I'm appreciating my loved ones more. My business is using the internet in more creative ways." When you question a stressful thought and turn it around, the thought loses its power over you, and the problems begin to disappear.

Whenever our thoughts are opposed to love, we feel stress, and that stress is a sign that we've drifted away from our original mind. If we feel balance and joy, that's a sign our thinking is more in line with our true identity, which is love. That's when we see the world as it really is: There are no mistakes. Whatever we get is what we need. And everyone and everything in life is here to wake us up.

The Lies in Your Head

Jewel is a Grammy-nominated singer, New York Times–bestselling author, and founder of the Inspiring Children Foundation. Cherrial enrolled in Jewel's mindfulness program in 2015.

⌒

JEWEL: I moved out at fifteen. My dad and I had a difficult relationship. There was abuse and alcohol in the home, and I knew at that time that I should end up a statistic, and I worried about nature versus nurture. If I didn't have good nurture, could I get to know my actual nature? Was happiness a learnable skill if it wasn't taught in my own home?

I set out to learn these things for myself and did pretty well until I was eighteen. Then I refused to sleep with a boss who propositioned me. When I turned him down, he wouldn't give me my paycheck, and I couldn't pay my rent. I started living in my car, then my car got stolen and I ended up in a vicious poverty cycle that caused me to be homeless for about a year.

It was about this time that I started having severe anxiety attacks, and I was shoplifting a lot. One day I was stealing a dress in a dressing room of a clothing store, and I saw my reflection in the mirror and realized I looked like a statistic. I decided to try to reverse engineer my way into my head by watching my hands, because your hands are the servants of your thoughts.

I didn't steal the dress. I walked out of the store. I decided I would take notes on everything my hands would do for two weeks, and the end result was my anxiety virtually disappeared. It was my first look into what I now call mindfulness. I began doing more investigations and experiments, just with myself, and it was one of the most productive and transformative years of my life.

At the end of that year, I was singing in a local coffee shop in San Diego and got discovered by a record company executive. And I made myself a promise that my number-one job in life would be to be a happy, whole human being. My number-two job in life would be to be a happy musician, singer-songwriter. So in 2002, I formed a youth foundation called Inspiring Children to teach kids the practices I began developing when I was homeless, practices that are now scientifically proven to work. I wanted to help the toughest cases, people who had no resources, people like me. The foundation has introduced me to remarkable young people, including Cherrial, who I met five years ago when she was fourteen, right when she got out of the hospital. She's going to tell some of her story.

CHERRIAL: Both my parents were addicts. At the age of thirteen, I tried to take my own life twice. When I was growing up, my dad either told me that I was his savior, or that everything was my fault and that I was the reason for his depression and addiction. Growing up was really confusing. I didn't know how to deal with my emotions and I had a lot of anger and hatred toward both my parents for the things they had done. Coming into Jewel's program, I learned about mindfulness and realized that I wasn't my negative thoughts and feelings, and I had the power to choose happiness in every moment. It allowed me to heal within myself, to let go of my anger, and it healed my relationship with my parents.

JEWEL: One of the most important things about mindfulness is realizing that not every thought and feeling is a fact. We don't have to believe all of it. One of the first exercises we started teaching you was about identifying all the lies in your head. I remember it was helpful for you to write down the lies and the truth.

CHERRIAL: Yes it was. Before I was able to sit down and meditate, the journaling exercise helped me create this separation from myself and my thoughts. Something you always say, Jewel, is "I am not my thoughts. I'm the observer of my thoughts." When I would journal, it made that a reality for me because I could physically see my thoughts on a sheet of paper, outside of myself. I realized that I wasn't my negative thoughts and feelings, and that created the separation I needed to detach and let go of them. It's been a gift, my second chance at life.

JEWEL: We all need a second chance sometimes, and we all need to make the most of it when we get it. What do we all want to get out of this time in quarantine? I want to share one more practice that might help you get what you want. It goes like this: There are only two basic states of being. There's dilated and contracted. Every thought, feeling, or action leads to one of those two states. One of the best hacks that I ever found for anxiety was becoming deeply grateful, because joy, gratitude, observation, curiosity—all these dilate your system, while anger, worry, fear, anxiety contract your system. That is a biochemical response. When we dilate, our blood pressure drops, and the blood flow patterns in our brain change.

I remember the first time I got this to work for me. I was standing on a street corner, back when I was homeless, and felt an anxiety attack coming on. I decided to become profoundly grateful. The trick is you need your whole body to feel it. It can't just be a mental thing. Your whole body has to be deeply stimulated by that emotion. I remember the sun was shining through a palm tree casting a beautiful shadow on my skin, and I became profoundly grateful that I was alive in that moment to feel it. It helped me ward off a panic attack for the very first time, and that was a really big deal for me— learning the power of gratitude.

No matter what we endure in life, we are never broken. If you want to try some of the exercises that have helped me heal, visit jewelneverbroken.com. It's work, but life is work no matter what, so why don't we work toward happiness?

Leaning into the Unknowing

Brie Stoner, a cofounder of UNITE, is a recording artist and musician, a published writer, a student of mysticism, and a cohost of Richard Rohr's podcast, Another Name for Everything, *at the Center for Action and Contemplation in Albuquerque, New Mexico.*

❧

All spiritual traditions teach that there is a deep connection between the personal and the social, between the practices of interiority and our life in society. Reverend angel Kyodo williams says, "Without inner change, there can be no outer change. Without collective change, no change matters."

So when we do our inner work, we're not just doing it for ourselves; we're doing it for the sake of the whole because it changes how we relate to each other. As we become more united within ourselves, we become more united as a society.

How do we do our inner work? Any practice that helps us create a blank slate, that helps us release the ways we cling to our stories and relax into a state of trust, is a positive practice. If I can let go of my assumptions, then I'm also able to let go of the ways I tend to put those assumptions on you. And when we let go of old narratives, we move more fully into the potential of what could be—for ourselves and for the world.

Many Christian mystics describe this as "leaning into the unknowing," which most of us don't enjoy. We're not comfortable not knowing, not being certain—especially in this crisis we're facing. It's difficult not knowing when we'll get back to a normal life, when we'll get back to our jobs, but this mystics' place of unknowing is a creative place to be. Artists know this intuitively; I can't write a new song if I'm thinking about singing the song I wrote before.

All of us need to lean into that capacity, to move into a state of unknowing—and to see it as a practice that we do for the sake of the whole, for the sake of meeting each other from an entirely new place where I'm not going to limit you by stories about your past, and I'm not going to limit myself by clinging to old thoughts. Instead, we're going to move into the future we hope for together, and emerge from this crisis a more united human family.

Two young men look out from the edge of a rooftop.
Minneapolis, MN, USA. June 2020.

Something Happened in Me, and I Began to Cry

Brian McLaren is a scholar, activist, and public theologian. A former college English teacher and pastor, he is a passionate advocate for "a new kind of Christianity," and is the author of many books, including The Great Spiritual Migration: How the World's Largest Religion Is Seeking a Better Way to Be Christian.

⁓

Many years ago, one of my four children was diagnosed with cancer. He's thirty-five now, but he was just six and a half then. He had daily chemotherapy for about three and a half years, and for the first ten months he was hospitalized for a few days every month because his immune system was compromised, and his little body would get life-threatening infections.

One evening after I had been at the hospital, I got home and picked up the mail, dumped it on the kitchen counter, and noticed the monthly newsletter of an organization for parents of children with cancer. I opened it up and started reading the names of children who hadn't made it through the month. As I read the list, something happened in me, and I began to cry.

I wasn't simply crying for myself, my wife, my son, or our family. I began to feel a deep, deep empathy for every parent who had lost a child, and then beyond that for every parent who was caring for a sick child, and then beyond that—in some way that I still can't put into words—my empathy opened up and expanded for everyone, everywhere. I felt that we were all one—all suffering the same grief, all feeling the same fears, and all of us held in this same great big bottomless love. It was like the architecture of my mind and heart and soul got rearranged, and it's never gone back to the way it was before.

My roots in the contemplative tradition say that changing our world begins by changing our minds, not simply changing what we think but changing *how* we think. In the hardest times, our old ways of thinking fail us. They're often what got us into the hard times to begin with—and seeing that failure can open us up to new ways of thinking.

A contemplative mind is one that sees things whole. If you divide, it seeks to unite. If you exclude, it seeks to include. If you blame, it seeks to understand and forgive. A reactive mind says "Who's at fault for this? Who can I blame? How can we get back to normal?" But a contemplative mind knows we can't return to the old normal. Our old normal was based on the lie that we are all little monads of self-reliance, living in an economy that will protect us from all evil if we just work a little harder and make a little more money. We can't afford to return to that lie. In the new normal that we can create together, we can live out a truth that we're all learning in our bones, thanks to this crisis. We are all connected. We're all in trouble, and our only way out is together.

Taking the Time to Look at the Sky

Reverend angel Kyodo williams Sensei is an activist Zen priest, author of the book Radical Dharma, *and founder of the Liberated Life Network.*

⌒

None of us have lived through this in our lifetimes, and so we need to be kind to ourselves and befriend the feelings and experiences that come up for us. That will, in turn, allow us to be more kind to the people who are living close to us in the home, spending more time with us than we're accus-

A child enjoys Children's Day. Nanjing, Jiangsu Province, China. May 2020.

tomed to. Maybe befriending the feelings that come with this virus will allow us to be more kind to the people we find ourselves in communication with across the digital waves; maybe it will allow us to be more kind to the people who seem different from us—people who we don't feel so connected to. Maybe it will help us see that we're going through this pandemic together so we can become more kind to each other.

I hope that you will take time for this—maybe even taking the time to look at the sky—and ask how you can show yourself more kindness, how you can pay greater attention to the yearning you hold inside of you.

Let's take just one minute to settle into our bodies and feel what it is like to hold a sense of quiet and spaciousness so that we can scan our own selves and slow down our own breath, our own being, our own body in this moment.

Begin by feeling a sense of connection to your own feet. If you're in a home, imagine yourself having your feet on the earth. If you have shoes on, doesn't matter. Just feel your feet and the sense of grounding and connecting. Then feel your seat, your buttocks connected to whatever seat you're on. If you're standing, feel the back of your body and, taking an in-breath, extend into the full length of your spine, your crown toward the sky as you allow the breath to settle in the belly. Now, exhale deeply, and drawing the breath in again, draw your shoulders up and out; allowing yourself to be openhearted and soft-bellied, extend out into your width, feel your sense of relationship with everyone and everything around you. Exhale again, and finally, take in a breath and drop the breath into the belly. We call that grounding ourselves in our center, connecting to our core, allowing our breath to rest in our bellies, perhaps noticing where that breath is, and simply allowing your attention to rest. I always add one last thing, which is: at whatever point you have found that place of rest, just draw the corners of your mouth up into a smile, recognizing that you are valued, we are connected, we are all loved.

All Within Me and Myself Within All

Swami Atmarupananda is a scholar, teacher, and monk of the Ramakrishna Order of India.

∽

Namaste. *Namaste* is a gesture which is much more recognized now during the pandemic as people are discouraged from handshaking. As you probably know, the phrase *namaste* means "salutations to you." It's based on the idea that "I salute the reality which is manifested as you"—that means the cosmic reality that manifests as this universe. It's manifesting as me, it's manifesting as you. And I recognize you as a manifestation of that infinite reality.

We are in a time of great difficulty for many people. People who have lost their jobs. People who can't pay their bills. People who are sick. People who are taking care of the sick. We can feel at a loss for how to help. One thing we all can do is to pray for others. So let us pray. I'll translate a Hindu prayer, four short lines, and give a short commentary. We will pray together.

May all beings cross over difficulties.

I didn't say may all beings be freed from difficulty because that doesn't happen in life. But may we have the power to get to the other side of whatever difficulties come in our path.

May all beings see that which is noble and uplifting.

We are what we put into our minds, so if we fill our minds with too much bad news, it destroys the peace of our minds and hearts. So let us know that which we need to know, but also look to that which is noble and uplifting.

May all attain right understanding.

In the midst of the difficulties, may I know what is true, what is good, so that I know what I can do for the welfare of all.

May all delight everywhere. May all rejoice everywhere.

In the midst of the difficulties, may I find the power to see past the difficulty to the joyous nature of reality itself. One way of doing that is to learn to still the mind. When the mind becomes stillness, I find in the midst of the stillness, the sense *I am.*

If we can come to the simple sense *I am* without definition, then we begin to sympathize with *all* expressions of *I am*—the cosmic *I am.* I feel all within me, and myself within all.

*A protester extends a bouquet of flowers toward police officers during a
demonstration for racial justice. Santa Monica, CA, USA. May 2020.*

Even if You Feel Powerless and Small

Dr. Martha Beck is an author, speaker, and life coach. Maria Shriver is a journalist, author, former First Lady of California, and founder of the Women's Alzheimer's Movement.

༝

MARIA: You've called this a moment of transformation. What do you mean by that?

MARTHA: The pandemic has broken a lot in our society, but that helps us see that a lot was broken already—the oppression in various political systems, the domination of the poor by the rich. When a pandemic brings our mortality into our faces, it becomes a chance for transformation.

MARIA: But there is a lot of fear out there. People have lost their jobs, can't pay their bills, can't put food on the table. How are they supposed to see this as a transformative moment as opposed to a paralyzing and terrifying moment?

MARTHA: We're not taught in our culture to handle things that die and are reborn. A lot of cultures see everything as a cycle, but we in this culture see everything as a straight line that shouldn't be interrupted. We don't know what to do when the crops are all gone and it's wintertime, and nothing seems to be going right. But traditional cultures teach us there are two jobs we have during these times.

The first is to survive physically, but not by trying to plan things out over a long period of time. We have to take very small steps and plan just a short way ahead. The second thing we have to do is grieve because we've all lost so much. We've lost expectations, we've lost loved ones, we've lost jobs, and to survive emotionally requires grieving. Both those things are necessary but we can't do either of them by ourselves. We need each other.

MARIA: If I'm grieving, but I want to come out of this pandemic feeling less alone, what are some things I can do right now?

MARTHA: The first thing is to go inward and accept whatever anger and anxiety you're feeling. The second thing is to reach outward by expressing what's going on with you and allowing yourself to show that vulnerability to others. The third thing is to reach out to help others even if you feel powerless and small. Any act that you do to help another person takes you from the position of victim, mentally, to the position of creator—and creativity is the way out of fear.

MARIA: How do you do that? How do you take this moment when you're frozen in your home and say, "I want to use this and become a creator."

MARTHA: At the start of the pandemic, I was asking myself a useless question over and over, "What's going to happen? What's going to happen?" I kept thinking that, and one day I thought, no, the real question is: "What am

I going to make of this?" And then a loved one said to me, "Even that's the wrong question. It should be 'What can *we* make of this?'" When you switch to "What can we make of this?" instead of "What's going to happen?" everyone becomes part of the field of creativity, and that's what fixes things.

MARIA: We want to unite the country, we want to unite the world, but that means we have to unite ourselves first, putting the pieces of ourselves together so we can go out whole. Correct?

MARTHA: Absolutely. And that takes going within and admitting what's going on inside us emotionally. We have to be honest in this time. Only the truth is strong enough to take us through this tragedy.

Could You Please?

Suze Orman is an American financial adviser who has written ten New York Times–bestselling books on personal finance.

⁓

M any of us are afraid. We're afraid for our health. We're worried a family member might get the virus. We're scared that we're not going to have enough money to feed our kids, or pay our bills.

Fear is the greatest internal obstacle to wealth. When you are afraid, you are paralyzed. You're thinking, "I can't do anything." The only way to conquer fear is through action, and I'm asking all of you to take action. If you owe people money, I want you to contact every single creditor, and simply ask them: "Could you please . . . ?" Those are the three greatest words in life. Could you please postpone my payments? Because there's never been a time when people are more willing to help. And if somebody says no to you, I want you to call back and call back, because every "no" in life leads you that much closer to a "yes."

And for those of you who still have a job, for those of you who have more than you need, this is the time to unite with all of us and give, give, give. Let the money flow in through your hands and out through your heart to make this world a better place for all.

We Are Not in Control

Charlamagne tha God is an author, speaker, and cohost of the national radio show The Breakfast Club. *Dr. Rheeda Walker is a licensed psychologist, a professor of psychology at the University of Houston, and the author of* The Unapologetic Guide to Black Mental Health.

∽

CHARLAMAGNE: It is okay to not be okay. But once you learn there are tools to help you be okay, then it's not okay to *stay* not okay. I want to give people tools to cope with their mental health issues during quarantine and after, and for me, telling your story is one of the best tools we have—not just in my community, the Black community, but throughout all of America. People have to tell their stories. But I'm very aware that when I say, "How are you doing?" I have to be ready to receive whatever story they tell me because it may not be all good for them. Dr. Walker, you talk about "the ABCs of support." Can you break that down?

DR. RHEEDA: I like the ABCs because they are straightforward. A is Assume you can help. We get overwhelmed if someone else is struggling. Suspend that for a moment and assume we can be helpful. B is Be a good listener. We never know what someone is going through. It is important for us to be able to listen and hear the other person. The C is Cancel your judgments. We can't think properly if we are judging someone.

CHARLAMAGNE: Canceling your judgments is hard because you don't want the person to harm himself, so should you always be quiet and listen the whole time and offer no advice?

DR. RHEEDA: The short answer is yes. When we put pressure on ourselves to try to fix what is going on for someone else, it makes it hard for us to listen. A lot of people who are struggling want and need to be heard. They want to feel like someone cares for them. Being able to listen goes a long, long way. We don't have to solve people's problems for them.

CHARLAMAGNE: For those of us who have always dealt with anxiety and have been told we make up things to worry about—what do you tell us when we actually *do* have something to worry about?

DR. RHEEDA: There are levels of worry. It can run from zero to twenty or seventy-five or a hundred. If circumstances call for worry to be at a fifty, but we take worry to a ninety, we may want to check those thoughts. One of the things we can do is write down our "worry thoughts" on paper to get some perspective so they don't get out of hand. Some teachers talk about the value of stillness, but a lot of us can't achieve stillness because of the thoughts in our head. If we can write down those thoughts, that can give us a lot of relief from worry we don't have to be experiencing and also give us space to problem-solve troubling situations.

CHARLAMAGNE: Why is having access to a higher power so important to mental health?

DR. RHEEDA: A higher power helps us recognize it is not all on us. We get anxious sometimes because we feel we should be in control of everything. The reality is we are not. That is why we are all at the house right now. We are not in control. When we can relinquish some of that to the universe, and say, "You know what, I'm going to stay over here, do my part, be safe at home, wear a mask, and let the universe heal itself." That helps with anxiety, I can sit back and relax a little bit. I don't have to worry about things that are out of my control.

CHARLAMAGNE: In your book, you talk about being genuine about needing help. What does that look like?

DR. RHEEDA: Being genuine is being your authentic self. There are so many of us walking around with what I call "our representative." There is the *real* us—who is a mess, or is struggling, or needs to learn something, or needs to sit down. Then there is "our representative" we present to the world—who has everything put together, doesn't need help, is not struggling. That representative is inauthentic. It's someone we have to work to create. When we can be our authentic selves, we can pick up the phone and reach out to a loved one and say we're having a tough time. It is okay to take a step back and say, "You know what, I am not going to be my representative. I'm going to be someone who needs to reach out to others and get help."

I Watched All My Friends Die

Lee Daniels is a writer and filmmaker known for directing the film Precious *and cocreating the television show* Empire.

When I was asked to offer my thoughts, I didn't know how I could help. I didn't know who I could touch. And then I realized I should talk about what started me on this roller coaster of addiction. And it was the AIDS epidemic some forty years ago. That was like living in the same space we are living in right now. It decimated the gay community, and particularly the African American gay community. I watched all my friends die, and I couldn't figure out why it had not taken me. So, I started using drugs, and it was a plunge into hell that I would not wish on my worst enemy. And so I have something to say to those people right now who are addicts and want to use, because this crazy mess that we're in right now will *make* you want to use. It will make people that *aren't* addicts want to use. For those fellow addicts, you're not alone. There are millions and millions of people who are just like us. Stay in the moment. Stay in the moment. We have no control over this. But it too shall pass. It too shall pass. So smile, you woke up this morning. God is good. Don't use, no matter what.

Saving Our Lives for Centuries

"Nap Bishop" Tricia Hersey is a performance artist, activist, theologian, and creator of the Nap Ministry, which advocates rest as resistance to burnout culture.

⌒

This is a call to rest. This is a call to slow down. This is a call for silence. This is a call for imagination, for collective care. This is a call to listen. A call to grieve. This is a call for slow, deep breathing. May we have a soft space to rest. May this space be in the physical and mental realm. May we ignore the rush to productivity. May comfort and ease pour over us like water. May we remember that radical care has been saving our lives for centuries. May deep rest come to you always. May we see the liberating power of rest as a foundation for a new world. May we see the beauty of a pause. May we daydream while imagining rest as a portal for healing. This is a call to rest.

We Are Loved, Loved, Loved

Amy Grant, the Grammy Award–winning singer-songwriter who put contemporary Christian music on the map in the 1970s, is a television host, speaker, philanthropist, and bestselling author of Mosaic: Pieces of My Life So Far.

༚

Years ago, I was in a hotel room around midday in Richmond, Virginia. I had a show that night, and I was going to spend the afternoon with a friend—but feeling responsible for what was going to happen onstage, I wanted to make sure that I was grounded.

I'm a person of faith, and so I read my Bible (Psalm 46:10 "Be still and know that I am God"; John 3:16 "For God so loved the world . . ."), and I prayed for the people who were coming to the show. When my friend Mel showed up, I told her, "I can't seem to do this. I'm trying to be still, and all my mind does is just rev more and more and more."

And, in an effort to invite her into the chatter of my brain, I started speaking out loud what was in my head. "Is it just me? Or do we all feel this way? I feel overwhelmed by life. I feel that the gifts that I bring are not enough." And I held out my hands palms up and started saying, "God, this is how we all live: overwhelmed, insecure, uncertain, fearful." And then I took a deep breath and said, "This is how we live, but this is who we are. We are loved."

And I said, "Mel, just for a minute, go with me. Let's just try this. I've got too much stirring in my head. I can't pray a succinct prayer, but if I can just lay my body down, prostrate my flesh and bones as a living prayer, if I can just tell my head 'shhh,' maybe I can surrender to the truth that we are loved." And I lay facedown on the floor for a breath, and got back up and said,

Family members mourn the death of Conrad Coleman, Jr.,
who died of COVID-19. New Rochelle, NY, USA. July 2020.

"How is your brain? Mine's revving even more, but at least I feel a camaraderie with you."

So, we began this pattern of saying, "This is how we live." And Mel and I took turns naming our chatter, and after we had both spoken, we said, "Okay, this is how we live. But this is who we are. Loved. Loved. Loved." And she and I went facedown on the ground for one breath. And then we stood back up, named the new chatter, and continued the pattern, prostrating and standing.

This is what I would like to invite you to do with me. I'm just going to name my chatter, and I would like you to name yours. I bet they're not that different. My chatter is fear of putting myself out there by sharing this practice with you, fear that I'll be made a fool of. That's some of my chatter. I'm afraid for my children. I'm filled with uncertainty. This is how we live, all of us. But this is who we are. We are loved, loved, loved.

Join me if you would like to, and speak whatever is your chatter. Because this is how we live: wondering if we're doing enough. This is how we live: full of longing, emotionally isolated, fearful. This is how we live: on an empty tank, flying by the seat of our pants, wasting precious time, not knowing what to do. This is how we live, all of us around the globe. But this is who we are. We are loved, loved, loved. Let your body be your prayer, prostrate and surrendered, and just say to yourself, "We are loved, loved, loved."

This pattern is my stillness practice. And if I allow that rhythm to happen as many times as it needs to—five, ten, fifteen—it will change what's happening inside. It always does.

You are loved.

Light Pouring from Your Heart

Gabrielle Bernstein is a number-one New York Times–*bestselling author and motivational speaker.*

༄

I've had a difficult experience, as we all have, being away from people and not feeling the connection that we have day to day. But that gives us the opportunity to develop a new practice—because sometimes we don't recognize the power of our energetic connection. When we set the intention to feel connected, we can align our energy to those we love. We can think of them and they may call. We can send them a prayer and they may answer with a text. My intention today is to ground us in a meditation that will unite us with the loved ones we have felt disconnected from, and also unite us as a community of like-minded souls who have come here at this time, in this way, to feel a connection and to unite completely.

I'd like to begin this meditation by asking you to place your left hand on your heart and your right hand on your belly. Inhale through your nose as you extend your diaphragm. Then exhale through your mouth, allowing the diaphragm to relax. Now gently close your eyes, continuing that cycle of breath. Call on the love and kindness that is supporting us. Accept that we can unite even if we are physically apart. Now set the intention to feel a greater connection to someone in your life you may feel disconnected from right now. Imagine them standing before you. Smile as you recognize their presence. Now breathe in the love that you have for this person, and on the exhale, extend that love from your heart to their heart. On the inhale, receive their love back to you, and on the exhale, see this golden chain of light pouring from your heart to theirs.

Continuing this cycle of breath, now extend that light far beyond this one person. On the inhale send it to somebody else and begin to receive it back. On the exhale you can send it out to the world. Visualize that light from your heart extending far beyond your physical sight to those who are needing your love, your connection. Breathe that space into your heart, and on the exhale send that light out to the world to all those who need it now.

When you see that golden chain of light extending from your heart to another's and then out to the world, you have an opportunity to deepen your connection to others, to align with a place of peace and extend that peace beyond your physical sight. This practice can help you feel centered, calm, more aligned. Let it be something you bring forth in your day-to-day life.

Who We Most Truly Are

Jessica Encell Coleman is a celebrator of life, amplifier of love, and the founder and creator of The Magic of Human Connection.

ॐ

Love is our greatest superpower. It is what the world most truly needs, and who each of us most truly are. I believe that love is the foundational nature of reality and that it exists everywhere at all times, just waiting to be enjoyed, expressed, and shared. I also believe that life is the most magnificent gift ever! That is why my absolute passion is creating experiences that bring people together to celebrate this gift of life and to cultivate the awe and joy and aliveness that comes from amplifying love. I am so excited to share one special way that you can experience the magic of amplifying love right now.

It's through a powerful practice called "Love Notes." A Love Note is a spontaneous video message of love, kindness, and encouragement, celebrating how much you treasure someone. It's a chance to make someone's day with the power of your heart. Creating a Love Note is simple, yet the impact can be profound.

Here's how: Close your eyes, and think of someone you are deeply grateful for. This could be someone you say "I love you" to every day and you just want to say it one more time. It could be someone you haven't talked to in a while who'll be surprised and delighted to hear from you. It could be anyone you want to express gratitude to. When you have this person in mind, take a deep breath and imagine the big, beautiful smile that will be on their face as they receive your unexpected love message. Now, record a video expressing your love and gratitude to this person and send it to them, feeling how you have brought even more love and connection into the universe.

Take a minute to notice how amazing that feels. Not only is the person receiving the Love Note getting a gift, but as you create it, you are getting a gift as well by opening even more to your inner joy and divine spark.

When we share the infinite abundance of love we have inside of us and send it out into the world, and when we feel the infinite abundance of love all around us and take it in fully—*that* is the greatest happiness and deepest fulfillment we can experience as human beings.

One of My Spiritual Goals

Angie Thurston is the cofounder of Sacred Design Lab and a fellow at the Harvard Divinity School.

∽

Even before the pandemic, we were already facing a crisis of isolation and loneliness, which wasn't about being physically apart; it was about a lack of meaningful connection to ourselves, our relationships, and our sense of purpose. Now many of us are facing that sense of disconnection and asking what to do about it—because people are realizing their sanity depends on connection. And we're identifying people in our inner circle and pulling them tighter, sometimes even releasing old grudges in order to do it.

One of my spiritual goals is to learn to love one new person every day. And this is a challenge in the best of times. Now it feels way out of reach. But that doesn't mean we can't focus our attention on love over fear. Fear is disempowering because it puts our attention on a future that we can't control, whereas love is empowering because it's something we can act on now. I've been wondering what this time would look like if we mark each day with an act of love. It might be a small thing like a text message to a friend or a note on a neighbor's door. Or it could be an act of self-compassion like a bath or a dance party. If there are acts of love you've been waiting to do, this could be the perfect time. If there is someone in your life you've been longing to get right with, you can be the one to reach out and say, "I want you to know I care too much to let this grudge be the last word."

*A nurse reacts to a Mother's Day performance by the Mexican
National Guard Orchestra. Monterrey, Mexico. May 2020.*

Sadness Is So Beautiful

Kasia Urbaniak is a practitioner of Taoist alchemy and founder of the Academy, a school that teaches women about the nature of power.

⁓

What comes up when we try to connect deeply? Often, it's conflict. We trigger in each other a stream of difficult emotions that none of us want to feel. But those negative, pesky, impossible emotions are actually tremendous gifts and potential allies. They can be alchemized into a resource of strength, clarity, power, and desire.

Let's take a feeling like sadness. Sadness is so beautiful. It usually begins with a story in the mind, and quickly starts sinking inward where all of our bodily sensations lie. Once there, it reveals some of our most tender, unspoken needs and desires. When we can access those tender needs, we are no longer paying attention to the thing that we want to get rid of. We're paying attention to the thing that we want to create more of.

Take another emotion, like fear. Nothing will help you access a desire faster than fear. If you are afraid of something, it's often because there is something even bigger that you want. Something is being threatened, and you want to protect it, you want to amplify it, you want to create more of it. So fear often exposes big, bold desires, things that are worth putting all of yourself into.

Take anger. Anger can be destructive. When you feel angry, everything comes up and out. You just want to shout. Often, because this energy is moving out, it looks for a target, something you're fighting against. The pivot is to move from what you're fighting against to what you're fighting for. This works well in close relationships because two people who are having conflict can sit down and go from fighting against each other to identifying what they're both fighting for, asking each other, "What is it this anger is trying to protect that we can create more of together?" Then the conversation can go from being destructive to being creative, to having possibilities that neither partner would have seen without first going through the pain.

A Turning Point in My Life

Lawrence Bartley is the director of News Inside *for the Marshall Project.*

‿

When I was seventeen years old, I went to prison. I was a scared teenager walking into an adult maximum-security facility, when just a short time before I'd been in the hallways of my high school, wearing eight-ball jackets and acid-wash jeans. I had traded my childhood for concrete prison yards and green uniforms that marked me as a dreadful person.

I had to learn how to adapt and survive while I was still a young boy who felt terrible for disappointing his family. As the years progressed, I gradually assimilated into my dismal environment. I tried to hold on to the core strength that was built by my grandmother's kisses, my father's mildness, and my mother's resilience. At the fourteen-year mark of my incarceration—just past the midpoint of my time in prison—I was lucky enough to be in a serious relationship with a woman who had a brilliant daughter. Despite my incarceration, this little girl clung to me like I was her dad.

One day during our many visits I sought to help her with her math. It wasn't that she couldn't do her math problems, it was just that it frustrated her. I wanted to help her clear her mind away from that frustration and think about new ways to solve the problems. I promised her that if she were to earn 100 on her next math exam, I would give her sixty dollars to buy her favorite sneakers.

At this time in prison, having sixty dollars in cash was against the rules. But I thought that if it would make this little twelve-year-old girl happy, then it was worth the risk. So I made a few cigarette exchanges and I raised the sixty dollars, and my plan was to hand it to her during our next visit. But when that day came, officers raided my cell, found the sixty dollars, and threw me into solitary confinement. Solitary confinement is a cell just a little bit bigger than a parking space. A person can stay there for months, and many times even years, with barely any access to natural light, and you can only get out of that cell for one hour a day.

Just after they put me in solitary, I was taken before a hearing officer who would decide if I were to be released or how long I would have to stay. I explained the story to him, telling him that the sixty dollars was intended as a gift in hopes that he would be lenient with me.

He heard me out, looked me in the eye, and sentenced me to *ten months* solitary confinement. I was shocked. I could barely get the words out to ask him why he had been so harsh. He looked me once more in the eye, this time with a touch of softness, and said, "Because it will make you stronger."

I went back to my cell dejected and broken. I barely even knew this guy. How could he determine what would make me better as a man? As time went on in my solitary cell, I experienced a deep sense of loneliness. The separation from others weighed on my mental health. So one day I just laid on my bunk and I began to think of everything in my life that went wrong, everything I had done that I wasn't proud of, everyone I had hurt. Then I decided to do the one thing that I could still do in my small cell.

I wrote letters to everyone, even those who wouldn't have the opportunity to read it. I didn't ask for anyone's forgiveness. I didn't ask anyone to write me back. This was about me being vulnerable, honest, and—most important—sorry.

I wanted to put it out there for those who deserved to read it. If I couldn't get my letter to them, I just hoped that somehow they would feel the energy that I was putting in the air. That marked a turning point in my life. I felt like I shed the chains of regret and selfishness that held me back. I got out of solitary confinement early. I progressed from a GED to a master's degree, I was published, I started a family—all while being incarcerated.

Upon my release, I embarked on a career at the Marshall Project, a non-profit newsroom that covers the criminal justice system. Incarcerated people, particularly those who are in solitary confinement, need high-quality information to inspire progress just as we do on the outside. So I founded *News Inside*, a print publication featuring stories that relate directly to incarcerated lives. We distribute it to people in prisons and jails across the country who struggle to find resources to expand their minds. When I was in prison and I saw friends go home, I always felt a surge of jealousy accompanied by a hope that my departing friends would not forget me. Now that I have been released, *News Inside* is my way of not forgetting them.

I hope that none of you go to prison, but right now we are all in a form of solitary confinement. Take the time to find a quiet place and ask yourself, "Is there anything in my life that is going wrong?" Ask yourself, "Are there any amends I need to make? Are there any regrets I could take this time to address?" Then take out a pen and a piece of paper and write a letter. It could be an email or a text, too, that'll do. You can write it to a group of people who you wronged. Or someone you didn't say goodbye to. Or a child you failed to encourage. You could even write it to yourself. Just say what you need to say.

Write without any expectation of a response, after you have taken the time to reflect on who you are as a person and what parts of your life are left undone.

The noise of the world is off. This is the best time to find yourself and reach others.

An Intravenous Dose of Hope

Kelly McGonigal is a health psychologist, dance-fitness instructor, lecturer at Stanford University, and bestselling author of The Willpower Instinct *and* The Joy of Movement.

Usually, I teach six dance classes a week. It's a tremendous source of joy and community in my life, so when we got the stay-at-home order over a month ago, I was pretty down. After a few days, though, I tried to restore that daily connection by filming classes and sending them to my students. Many of them have told me that being able to dance has given them a moment of joy in a confusing time. The same is true for me. Choosing to dance and to move is one of the sources of meaning I call on when I'm feeling alone and uncertain. Today I want to share with you five ways that moving your body can be a source of resilience in difficult times.

The first way is called the "feel-better effect." When you move your body, it immediately gives you more energy and optimism, in part because as soon as you start moving you get a burst of adrenaline and dopamine that just makes you feel better. The second is connection. When you move with other people, whether you are walking or running or dancing or lifting weights, it strengthens bonds and increases a sense of belonging. The third has to do with music. Music activates the motor system of the brain to give you a sense of joy in moving. Moving your body allows the energy of a song to get inside of you. If you move to music that makes you feel fierce, it brings out courage. If you listen to music that makes you feel happy, it brings out joy. Your playlist could be one of your greatest resources right now. The fourth way that movement can be a source of resilience is tied to "hope molecules." When you contract your muscles in any form of movement, it releases molecules into your bloodstream that travel to your brain, where they help relieve depression and anxiety. Every time you choose to move, you are giving yourself an intravenous dose of hope. The last way has to do with dancing. In every culture around the world, traditional dance forms are made up of movements that express and evoke joy. Whether you are bouncing, stomping, or spinning, these movements allow you to tap into the natural human capacity to celebrate life.

Moving my body has always been a way for me to deal with stress and anxiety and tap into my desire to give something to the world. When you choose to move your body, you are giving yourself permission to choose joy, even in the midst of chaos or pain. So get your dancing shoes on, and let's move!

Ballet dancer Ashlee Montague performs in a nearly empty
Times Square. New York, NY, USA. March 2020.

The Medicine of Sound

Medicine Woman gina Breedlove is a vocalist, composer, author, and sound healer.

 ⌒

I teach folk how to use the sound and vibration of their voices to bring themselves to the present moment, and I want to invite you to try it. I'm going to ask you to bring your hands to your mouth and speak a word into your palms, and see how the vibration and the sound of your voice can bring calm to your body.

Draw in a deep breath, and as you exhale, say "joy" into your palms five times. Feel the vibration of the sound of your voice moving the energy into your body. Notice how your voice in your body brings you to a still point. See how it can disrupt a narrative of fear. If we can replace fear with joy, we can share this medicine with those who aren't able to take a deep breath in this moment. Yes, we can breathe for each other. This is the magic of the medicine of sound, the medicine that you walk with.

There Is a Place Inside of Us

Arianna Huffington is the cofounder of The Huffington Post *and the founder and CEO of Thrive Global.*

⌒

Transformational change rarely happens without a crisis. The truth is that even before this pandemic began, we were already in the middle of a mental health crisis. Today, the loss of loved ones, the loss of jobs, financial insecurity, and long periods of isolation are making our lives infinitely harder. And just as we're making drastic changes to our lives to stop the spread of the virus, we need to take steps to safeguard our mental health, too.

I want to share my three favorite microsteps to help strengthen mental resilience. The first is whenever you are feeling overwhelmed during the day, instead of getting your phone and scrolling through social media, stop and take sixty seconds to focus on your breath. This grounds us in the present moment.

The second is deciding at some point at night to stop consuming news. We all want to stay informed, but it is important to get some truly recharging sleep. And when we are stressed out right to the very end of the day, without any transition before bed, it is much harder to sleep well.

The third step is gratitude. Gratitude is the most important antidote to our anxiety. At different times during the day, I try to remember three things that I'm grateful for. They don't have to be big things. Even little things can reduce stress and help us focus on what is working, what we love, what brings us joy.

These are three ways we can shift our culture away from a perpetually stressed-out fight-or-flight state and reconnect with essential truths. I'm

Greek, and all Greek philosophers—and indeed all philosophers and spiritual teachers everywhere—have said the same thing: there is a place inside us of peace, wisdom, and strength. It is as close to us as our next breath. We just need to pause and tap into it. And from that place, we will be so much stronger to deal with all the challenges ahead.

Magic Enters the Room

Donna Hicks, PhD, is an associate at the Weatherhead Center for International Affairs at Harvard University and has spent years working in conflict resolution in the Middle East and other high-conflict regions. She is the author of Dignity.

ᄋ᠆

Working as a conflict resolution specialist has given me many opportunities to meet with people who've been through trauma and are trying to heal. And the most important lesson I've learned is that when people understand what's happened to them through the lens of their dignity, they can make tremendous progress in recovering a sense of self-worth.

Dignity is our inborn value, our inherent worth. Our longing for dignity is the single most powerful human force motivating our behavior, in some cases even stronger than our desire for survival. Our dignity is honored when we feel we belong, when we feel acknowledged for our pain, when we feel safe, treated fairly, and in control of our lives.

The coronavirus pandemic has wounded the dignity of millions of people. When we lose our jobs or income, when we can't afford rent and need help getting food, we experience deep violations of our dignity. And it compounds the pain if we find it hard to talk about it.

Under normal circumstances, if I ask a group about a time they felt emotionally wounded, everyone remains silent. But as soon as I frame the question in terms of "violations to their dignity," everything changes. As my colleague Federica Vegas puts it, "it feels as if magic enters the room and everyone is suddenly able to speak."

Understanding our suffering in terms of wounds to our dignity not only gives us a way to talk, but it can show us how to help. We may not be able to help someone heal physically or financially, but we can help heal the wounds to their dignity by acknowledging the suffering they're going through, helping them regain some control, reassuring them it's not their fault, offering kindnesses that show them they matter.

Honoring dignity is at the core of many of the good deeds that touch our hearts. When we see doctors and nurses putting themselves at risk to heal the sick, they're honoring the dignity of people in need. When our hearts break for people, we feel the wound to their dignity, and it strikes at our own dignity as well. When we have the feeling that we're all in this together, we're feeling the dignity of something larger than ourselves. Dignity is our deepest need, and honoring each other's dignity is the path to unity.

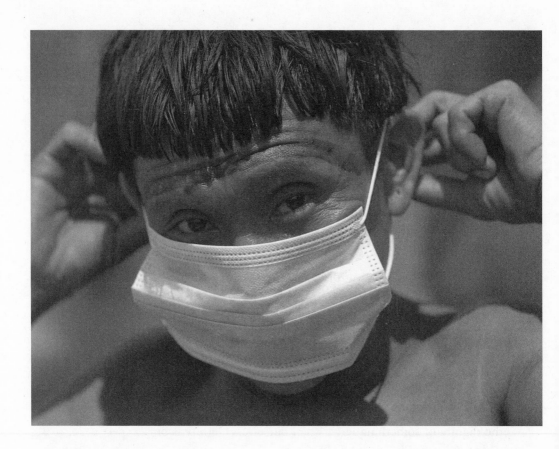

A man from the indigenous Yanomami ethnic group adjusts his protective mask. Alto Alegre, Brazil. July 2020.

Make Ourselves into
Something Better

Oprah Winfrey is an American talk-show host, producer, media executive, philanthropist, and author.

⁓

Since the pandemic took hold, I've talked to so many people I respect, and they're all saying the same thing: "We have been sent to our rooms for a time-out." We've been put on hold to look at ourselves. And I think our job during this time-out is to make ourselves into something better. That's what I'm trying to do—use the time to come out better on the other side.

One of the things we need to start doing, and I caution myself with this as well, is to be careful of the language we use to describe where we are and where we're going. I choose to stay positive. I choose to focus on all the people who are aligned in the hope and the work for a better world.

Forget about what we see on the news. We should turn it off. In this age, everybody gets caught up in the partisanship of one political organization or another, and the media is equally hysterical. If you leave it on all the time, you will be overwhelmed by the constant angst it brings into your home and spirit.

I focus instead on acts of courage and determination, stories of people who don't give up when they're hit with difficult times, but continue on and do their best to take care of their families and reach out to others.

Emphasizing the positive and being present in everything I do is what is getting me through. A few weeks into it, it dawned on me: I'm in my sixties, I had pneumonia last year, I have a preexisting condition, I'm in that category.

And it would have been overwhelming if I'd been following the spread of the virus, watching the news, the death toll, how many people in my city got sick or died. My favorite Bible verse, when I have seen too much news, is "In God I move and breathe and have my being." I repeat that, and I keep coming back to the present moment. Right now, my feet are on the floor, I am sitting in a chair, I am breathing good air, my lungs are working, I am well.

This is a time for our inner work, learning again that stress is wanting the present moment to be something it's not. As soon as we can accept what's going on and stop wanting to be somewhere we're not, things will get better.

This is also a time for our outer work. We're seeing tragic inequalities, and we're finding out who's really important, and it's not who we thought. Certainly, nobody looks at a grocery store worker the same again. Nobody looks at a deliveryman the same again. Previously invisible men and women have now got the title of "essential."

And every day as I wake up, I am thinking about the people who don't have what they need. I think every day how challenging it must be for families who have four kids at home and don't know how they will make it to the end of the month.

I was struck by the story of the African American son who lost his father and his grandfather in the same week. His father had gone to three different hospitals in Detroit trying to get treated, telling them he had the disease, and they wouldn't admit him.

So I believe it is a responsibility to use what we have—monetarily, socially, culturally, emotionally—to offer to those who don't have. As I was going through my closet the other day, I was thinking, what does this mean now? All the things we put on to show our status in the world, look who I am, look what I can have—all of that means nothing. That is what this time-out—

being sent to our rooms by the forces of life—is pushing us to do, to see ourselves and each other differently.

We're spiritual beings having a human experience. That I fundamentally know to be true. And we lose sight of our connection to each other and to the spiritual because we get so wrapped up in all the stuff of the world. What this moment is allowing us, even those of us who are in challenging circumstances, is to see the world differently. And I'm grateful for the lesson. Isn't all life experience here to show us who we are?

Who You Really Are

Jack Kornfield is a bestselling author, peacemaker, and Buddhist vipassana meditation teacher.

൦

When people are suffering, their pain is never separate from us—no matter where we live. It touches our hearts and our bodies because we are all in that field of caring for one another, whether we like it or not.

We know from research that even preverbal children care about those around them. If somebody is hurt, if another child is crying, if something gets lost, they want to help. That is born into all of us. It's what allows our species to survive. Even if we get frightened or confused, we all have the heart of compassion. When a baby is born, our first response is to love them. And when a loved one dies, our last gesture is to hold their hand. This timeless love is what really matters. And so part of what happens during painful times is that grief and anxiety build up in us. And we all wonder, "How do I find a way to hold this with a wise heart?"

So here is how I try to hold it all when I sit in meditation, or just sit quietly at the end of the day: Let yourself quiet down. And let your attention bring your body and mind together. If you are comfortable, let your eyes close. And notice with the kindest attention the state of your body. You can notice the areas of tightness, of tension that you carry, the fight, flight, or freeze response, the anxiety—it is all stored in the body.

And as you notice all that your body has been carrying, let yourself feel it quietly and tenderly, and wrap it with compassion. Because your body has been trying to protect you and carry you through this difficulty. And with your compassion, you can say thank you. Thank you for trying to protect me. I'm okay for now. What matters is that I am present, alive, and can love. Then you start to think about those you care about, and the beautiful thing is to ask your heart, what is your best intention in this time? And your heart will talk to you. As you listen to that response from the heart, it will lead you back to what you can offer and live from. From there, your body can soften and sense that you are okay, that there is something bigger than all the fears and all the tensions that you carry, and that is the space of love, and that is who you really are.

IV.

No Boundaries Are Real

SEEING UNITY IN HUMANITY

There is a simple proof that we are one: It hurts when we're divided, and we feel whole when we're united.

In part IV, we hear the voices of Muslims, Jews, and Christians, of poets, activists, and astronauts, of gay, straight, and trans people all bearing witness to unity—within ourselves, in all created things, and with God.

Anousheh Ansari talks about the false lines on maps dividing countries. Father Greg Boyle talks about the false lines in society separating humans. Rabbi Marc Gellman says human beings were made so we could finish creating the world together with God.

In this world we're creating together, nobody has to fit in—because everybody already belongs. Unity is not the opposite of diversity. Unity *requires* diversity. Without diversity, it's not true unity.

North and South America at night, assembled from data acquired by the Suomi NPP satellite. April and October 2012.

When we understand that happiness comes from unity, and unity is fulfilled by diversity, then we can't help but prepare a place for everyone. That's what moves Rabbi Abby Stein to say "bring them in." That's why Lamont Young serves as a counselor in a homeless shelter in the time of COVID. They find themselves when they unite others.

Unity is the truth of Sacred Scripture. It's the truth of oral traditions of indigenous peoples. It's the truth written in our hearts that we can test in our lives: when we feel separate, we suffer. That's why we find happiness in belonging. We are one. No one can be left out. We were made to be together.

We're Not Separate

Peggy Whitson was the first female commander of the International Space Station and has spent 665 days in space, making her NASA's most experienced astronaut. Rusty Schweickart was the lunar module pilot on the 1969 Apollo 9 mission, the first crewed flight test of the lunar module. Anousheh Ansari was a space flight participant who traveled to the International Space Station in 2006. George Whitesides is the CEO of Virgin Galactic, an aerospace and space travel company.

⁓

RUSTY: I flew on Apollo 9 back in 1969. We spent ten days in orbit testing the lunar module before my buddies, four months later, landed it on the moon and first set foot on that planet. That experience of ten days in space, and looking at the beautiful Earth that supports all of life, changed the ways I look at this planet and at life itself.

I can't describe how special it is when you look down on the Earth from space. It's an amazingly beautiful planet that we live on, and you realize that Earth is not only a spaceship on which we are crew and not passengers, but it's also Mother. We are being born into the cosmos. All of us together are life on this planet. When you ponder that, you begin to realize how precious we all are. We're not separate when you look down from space. And the challenge we're facing right now requires us to see that we can't survive as individuals; we've got to take care of not only the spaceship, but all the other crew members as well.

ANOUSHEH: I love what Rusty said. As we grow up, we're shown these lines that separate countries on a map, and we're tricked into believing that we're separated from each other—that "our" problems are different from "your" problems. But when you see our beautiful world from space, you understand that those lines are not real. We are all connected.

GEORGE: When astronauts are up in space, they are utterly remote from the rest of humanity. There are a lot of people who are feeling alone now. Is there any advice you might want to share with people who feel isolated?

PEGGY: My advice is to keep the big picture in mind. When I was cleaning the walls or fixing the toilet on the International Space Station, I'd focus on the big picture, and that's being part of space exploration. I think during this pandemic, the big picture we have to think about is saving lives. COVID-19 is showing us that we are all one planet, that we all share the same air, good or bad, and we have to deal with things together.

RUSTY: I'm reminded of the question, "Am I my brother's keeper?" We *are* all brothers and sisters on this planet together. How each of us acts affects all of us, but it also affects the future. It seems clear to me that we are one another's keepers. We've got to love and take care of the spaceship and one another. That, to me, is the big picture.

The Web of Life

Sherri Mitchell is an Indigenous rights activist, lawyer, spiritual teacher, and author of Sacred Instructions: Indigenous Wisdom for Living Spirit-Based Change.

⌒

I'm being called by my children and my grandchildren to share a story with you from our oral tradition, our story of the first illness.

The human beings, the two-leggeds, had fallen out of alignment with the path of life. And because they had fallen out of alignment with the path of life, they'd lost their ability to understand the language of the animals. They'd lost their capacity to hear the tiny voices of the trees and the plants. And so they began behaving in ways that were destructive to other species, and the other species were starting to talk about what they were going to do about the humans.

After living with the destructive ways of the humans for generations, the animals finally came together in council and decided that the only way to allow the human beings to recognize that they are connected to the rest of life is to give them illness so they can start to see how their destructive ways are causing harm.

So the human beings began to get sick. They began to die from the illness that was given to them by the animals. After watching them suffer for a time, the trees and the plants came together again in council, this time feeling grief and compassion for the human beings, and decided that, if they could get a message to the human beings and if the human beings were capable of receiving the message, they would give them the medicine they needed to heal themselves.

So that message was formulated and was sent to the human beings by the wind bird, and the message was received in a dream by one of the elders in the human community. Upon waking, the elder went to the forest and humbly asked the trees and the plants to help her. She asked the animals to forgive her. She asked Mother Earth to guide her. For days and days, she went back and made offerings and humbly asked for help, and finally the trees and the plants began to speak to this grandmother. And they gave her the wisdom that she needed to heal her people.

The grandmother then carried the medicine back to the human beings, and they took the medicine and began to become well again. And the grandmother told them the story of her dream, and her experience of reconnecting with the natural world, and recognizing the place that humans hold in the larger scheme of creation. And the humans decided that they would go back and live in deeper relationship with the natural world, that they would walk away from the life of distraction that kept them from hearing the words of the animals and the voice of the trees.

Many of us around the world are feeling immense grief, experiencing deep loneliness, waking up with panic in the middle of the night. When we understand the web of life, we start to understand that we are feeling the experience of other life forms on the planet. When we're with family and begin to feel immense loneliness, we can recognize we are feeling the loneliness of the last northern white rhinos on the planet; we're experiencing the panic of the trees as the fires and the loggers come toward them in the Amazon; we're experiencing the grief and loss of the mother whale who carried her dead baby calf with her for seventeen days trying to show us what we're doing to their ecosystem.

When we understand the depth of our connection, we start to understand that some of the experiences we're having during this time are evidence that something is being righted within us as a species. We are being reconnected with life. We have an opportunity now to re-member all the parts of who we are, to answer the call of the animals, to answer the call of the trees, and the plants, and the water, and the air and soil of Mother Earth. We have the opportunity now to answer the call of future generations who are asking us for the opportunity to be born into a world that can sustain them.

A Call Back to the Land

John Gourley and Zachary Carothers are members of Grammy Award– winning band Portugal. The Man. Chief Roberto Múkaro Borrero is a human rights advocate, author, and leader of the Guainia Taino Tribe.

ZACH: As we develop vaccines and treatments for this virus and we all start to feel safer, we're going to have the opportunity to build a new world, and I think a big part of that is hearing a call back to the land. That's why we are trying to raise up indigenous voices.

CHIEF: You've been doing some great work for others when you were able to be on the road. Can you share a little bit about "land acknowledgment" and what that means?

ZACH: We grew up very close with the native Alaskan community, and the culture is all about respecting the land and the people of it. Everywhere we go, we like to share the stage with indigenous peoples of the area who have been the stewards of that land forever, or have been displaced there. We invite them up and pass the mic. It's a shared learning experience between us and the crowd. We get to learn about the land that we are on, the place where we are connecting and having a good time. It's a way to elevate indigenous voices.

JOHN: In doing that, everyone gets to be educated together. We didn't always know what we know. Someone taught us. Now we're sharing the stage with the people whose land we're on so they can teach others.

CHIEF: Is there anything we can all do to help us move through this in a good way?

ZACH: I would like all of us to recognize the power we have. I don't mean the power of people following you on social media, or the power to make money or control others. I mean the power to change ourselves, and by changing ourselves to change the world. The virus has given us time to think about the kind of world we want. It has also forced us to act for the benefit of those around us—to wear masks and follow protocols and isolate ourselves because we don't want our friends, our elders, our neighbors to get sick. Everything we do, especially now, we do for the folks around us. And we can carry that forward. We can create the world we want to walk into when this is done.

CHIEF: The world you want to create elevates the voice of indigenous peoples. This is what we have been calling for, a seat at the table. If you don't have a seat at the table, you are probably serving those who are, or you are on the menu. We want to thank you for giving us a seat and a voice.

I Will Be Your Partner

Rabbi Marc Gellman is rabbi emeritus of Temple Beth Torah in Melville, New York. He is known for appearing on the television program The God Squad, *and is dedicated to interfaith religious discussion.*

ᘒ

Someday there will be a medical vaccine to protect us from the virus. But right now, what we need is a spiritual vaccine to protect us from fear. It won't protect us from suffering. God does not promise us—in any of the faiths I know—a life without suffering. God promises us a life where we need not fear and we need not suffer alone, because God is with us.

There is a story I wrote years ago—a story about a story in the Bible. The Hebrew word for this is *midrash*, which means textual interpretation. This is a *midrash* for children about the story of the creation of the world.

Before there was anything, there was God and a few angels and a huge swirling glob of rocks and water with no place to go, and the angels asked God, "Why don't you clean up this mess?" So, God collected the rocks from the huge swirling glob and put them together in clumps and said, "Some of these clumps of rocks will be planets and some will be stars and some of these rocks will be just rocks." And the angels asked, "Is the world finished?" And God said, "Nope," or words to that effect.

So God collected the water from the huge swirling glob and put it in pools, and God said, "Some of these pools will be oceans, and these will be lakes and these will be rivers and these will be clouds and some of this water will be just water." And then the angels asked, "Is the world finished?" And God answered again, "Nope," or words to that effect. On some of the rocks God placed growing things and creeping things and things that only God knows what they are, and the angels asked again, "Is the world finished?" And God said, "Nope," or words to that effect.

And then God made a man and a woman and said to them, "I'm tired now, please finish the world for me. It's almost done." But the man and the woman said, "We can't finish the world alone. You have the plans and we're too little." "Oh, you're big enough," God answered them. "But I'll agree to this: If you keep trying to finish the world, I will be your partner."

The man and the woman asked, "What's a partner?" And God said, "A partner is someone you work with on a big thing that neither of you can do alone. If you have a partner, it means that you can never give up because your partner is depending on you, and on the days that you think I'm not doing enough, I'm still your partner, and on the days that I think you're not doing enough, you're still my partner. We must not stop trying to finish the world together."

Then the angels asked God, "Is the world finished now?" And God answered, "I don't know. Go ask my partners."

Community members show support for long-term care facility workers. New Hope, MN, USA. April 2020.

Bring Them In

Rabbi Abby Stein is an author, speaker, activist, and rabbi. She is the first openly transgender woman to have been raised in an ultra-Orthodox Hasidic community and the author of Becoming Eve: My Journey from Ultra-Orthodox Rabbi to Transgender Woman.

❧

You don't need me to tell you we need to be connected, because we *are* connected. If people try to say we are divided, nature sends an enemy that *proves* that we're connected.

In this time of physical distancing, though, we have an opportunity to get socially closer than ever before by bringing in people who do not have spaces where they feel welcome. This is common among LGBTQ activists, among people of different faiths, among people who come from different countries, different backgrounds, people who suffer hate for who they are, or suffer hate for who they love. We have a chance now to create communities that don't know any borders because the internet doesn't need borders, and our love doesn't *have* borders.

I am putting out a call to each one of you—and also to myself and to my loved ones—to create social communities that are closer than ever before. In Judaism, we believe that prayers and acts that we do together have more power than acts that we do alone. So, whenever we sit down to eat a meal, or to watch a movie, I want us to think of the people who might not have access to these spaces, access to these abilities, and I want us to go out of our way to make sure we bring them in.

I am hoping right now, as we listen to people from all across the world, from across different spectrums, that we take action—not just in calling for unity, but in taking actions for unity. Next time you host an online event, or when it's a physical event in the future, go out of your way to think of who you wouldn't have invited otherwise, and bring them in.

There Will Be Heard Again the Voice of Mirth

Greg Boyle is a Roman Catholic priest of the Jesuit order and founder of Homeboy Industries, the world's largest gang-intervention and rehabilitation program. As a graduate and now trainee at Homeboy Industries, David Piña mentors former gang members. Jessica Sanchez, the organization's Government Relations assistant, is also a graduate of the program. Chris Miller is a member of the Homeboy Industries community.

⁓

FATHER GREG: Our goal is to stand with the demonized so that the demonizing will stop, to stand at the margins because that's the only way they'll get erased, to stand with the disposable so that the day will come when we stop throwing people away. We believe that the measure of our compassion lies not in our service of those on the margins, but in our willingness to see ourselves in kinship with them.

The prophet Jeremiah writes, "In this place of which you say it is a waste, there will be heard again the voice of mirth and the voice of gladness. The voices of those who sing." In this time of pandemic, we want to hear the

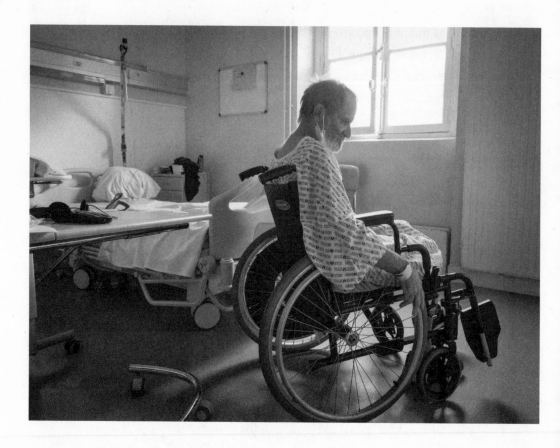

Gerard Guerin, a recovering COVID-19 patient experiencing homelessness, at the Henri Vidal Hospital. Paris, France. April 2020.

voices sing again. So we imagine a circle of compassion, and we imagine nobody standing outside that circle. We imagine communities who stand in awe at what the poor have to carry, rather than stand in judgment at how they carry it.

JESSICA: After about a month on lockdown, I started going through a lot of stuff with the girls. Ever since I barely got them back, I never took the time to slow down with them. I started realizing that I didn't really know them, so I began spending more time with them. Cooking has been everything for us. Every single time we start cooking, we bond. We argue for a bit, but when we sit down and eat, it's the best.

DAVID: I'm trying to open up more in relationship with my children, with my fiancée, with my family members, and with the Homeboy family, while connecting with my therapist and other people who are staying in contact with us. I look at it like this is helping me grow better as a man so I'll know what to do when we come out of quarantine.

CHRIS: I miss so many of the people who make a big difference in my life. It's hard for me to change because I don't see them as often. I've been telling my brothers and sisters that I stay by, even though they want us to quarantine, we still have to reach out to the ones we care about. We still got to stay connected. The only thing we can do is overcome this with love.

When They Counted Him Out, You Counted Him In

Lamont Young, a cofounder of UNITE, is a therapist, mental health activist, and survivor of gun violence. His mother, Glenda Sherrod, is an ordained minister.

∽

TIM SHRIVER: When I was a young kid just out of college, I was teaching and working at Hillhouse High School in New Haven, Connecticut. We had a lot of students who faced the dangers of guns and gangs, and we started a leadership group with some of the guys who wanted to work hard to beat the odds. We focused on problem solving, and keeping it safe. One morning, I arrived at school and heard one of our kids had been shot, and I ran to the principal to find out who it was. "Lamont Young," he told me. "Is he one of yours?"

"*Lamont?* That's not possible!" I said.

The principal gave me a look that said he knew the brutality of our kids' world and he wasn't sure I understood it yet. "They shot him seven times at point-blank range, Tim. He's still alive, but I don't know how long he'll last."

When I arrived at the hospital room, there was a police officer standing outside the door. He let me pass, and I saw Lamont wrapped in bandages, hanging on to life. I talked to him and got no response, so I sat and held his hand. When I was getting ready to go, I saw he was trying to say something, and I leaned in and heard him whisper, "Shrivs, next time I'll use problem solving."

Lamont, you and I have talked about this over the years, but when your life was hanging in the balance, how did you find the strength to come back? And where did you find the willingness to make peace with the person who wanted to kill you?

LAMONT: Beginning when I was two years old, my mother brought me up in Bible study, so I understood the power of forgiveness. My friends wanted me to retaliate, but that spiritual teaching allowed me not to cross that line.

TIM: That was your influence, Minister Glenda. So many children grow up and hear religious teachings, but they don't sink in. What do you think allowed Lamont to face this violence but not fight back?

GLENDA: The book of Proverbs tells us, "Train up a child in the way he should go, and when he is old he will not depart from it." When I was young, my mother, who is very spiritual, taught me the way of forgiveness, and I passed it on to my children down through the years. When you learn to forgive others, you also forgive yourself.

I thank God that Lamont is alive today, because he caught seven bullets and he was laying there in the street dying. Lamont knew the Scripture, though, and he was on the ground saying, "No weapons formed against me shall prosper." When I think about it, it brings tears to my eyes. I thank God for you, Tim. You saw Lamont's worth. What no one else saw, you saw. When they counted him out, you counted him in.

TIM: It was easy to see a lot in Lamont, Minister Glenda. I can't take any credit for that. Lamont, you're working with men right now who don't have homes, don't have incomes. They need the support and service that you're providing them. But how do we end the causes that are keeping us so divided? You're in the clinical world. How can the skills of a therapist help us now?

LAMONT: We need to understand trauma-related dissociation. We need to understand that we can become disconnected through situations that happen in our lives, and the best way to approach people who are detached from themselves is to help them embrace their realities slowly—to let them know that, together, with love, we can walk this path toward healing.

Connects Us to All Life

Mona Haydar is a poet, activist, chaplain, and rapper known for her protest song "Hijabi." Mirabai Starr is an author, speaker, bereavement counselor, and teacher of interspiritual dialogue. Reverend Jennifer Bailey is an ordained minister, public theologian, and founder and executive director of the Faith Matters Network.

∽

MIRABAI: I'm a Jewish woman with a Hindu guru, a Buddhist meditation practice, and a Sufi heart who loves Christ and Mother Mary, and I have been embracing this time of the pandemic as a Sabbath space. In my ancestral tradition of Judaism, this is the most sacred space there is, Shabbat, which begins tonight with the kindling of the Sabbath candles and lasts until Saturday night at sundown. There is something about the quality of this time we're finding ourselves in that feels like a collective Sabbath, whether we chose it or not. Most of us, of course, would not choose to be cut off from the things that ordinarily sustain us, but here we are. That's how it is in Judaism. It's a mitzvah to observe the Sabbath, to keep the Sabbath holy, and a mitzvah is both something you are supposed to do, like a responsibility, and also an invitation and a blessing. So that's how I'm approaching this time, as an opportunity to go inward, to—in Heschel's words—build "a palace in time" and enter in. So I want to share with everyone the beautiful Sabbath blessing that this time can become for us—and I get, by the way, that it's a privilege to be able to embrace this as a sacred time when so many people on the front lines and on the margins are suffering.

MONA: I am the daughter of diaspora. I have Damascene roots, born in the Arabian Peninsula and raised in Flint, Michigan, on Anishinabek land. In Flint, I was Arab and Muslim, neither Black nor White. Growing up, I didn't see any reflections of myself around me. The pain of not seeing myself represented caused me to search for the truest definition of self. Where could I find "me"? At twenty-three, I suffered a tragedy that sent me to the top of a mountain in northern New Mexico. There, I found myself reflected in all the heavens and Earth. Gazing up at the clear New Mexican night sky, I felt my ancestors and the ancestors of that land call me in and tell me that I am a daughter of all worlds; and, should I seek to serve and beautify the world through the gift of my life, I would find what I was looking for. It was during loss that I learned I could drink from the mystical well of traditions which says, God is everywhere, even closer to me than the blood flowing in my veins.

Demonstrators gather at a memorial to George Floyd.
Minneapolis, MN, USA. June 2020.

During this pandemic, I notice that I'm forgetting to breathe. I find I haven't taken a real deep breath all day. In realizing this, I find more groundedness, and I arrive at steady deep breaths through the word *Allah*. The breathy vibration it creates in my chest fills me with a symphonic and organic rhythm, like the beat of an ancient drum. "Allah" has been my mantra during this time. This ancient word which Abraham, Mary, and Jesus also used in calling upon the Divine, is the same word which grounds me in 2020. Strange how it is now a word which has been so vilified and weaponized, which a young Muslim in Flint felt unsafe uttering in her high school cafeteria. I remember sitting there, whispering the words "Bismillah" ("*in the name of Allah*") before I ate, fearful that someone might hear. Overcoming my own fear of rejection, I knew I was supposed to breathe deep, speak God's name, take a moment in prayer, deepening into stillness and embracing conscious breath in my life. I chose as a young woman to be Muslim and to say *Allah* out loud and to breathe deeply. The more I take time to breathe consciously, embracing the fullness and complexity of myself, the more I realize that I am connected to everything and everyone in ways that are ineffable. I am unable to capture this Divine dance of entanglement between myself and everything else with words, but breath, deep breath, somehow captures it. In this time, the word, the breath, *Allah*, is my radical act of rebellion, my connection to the collective through all space and time.

REV. JEN: Mona, the idea of breath as a revolutionary act is so resonant for me in my own lived experience of faith, as a minister in the African Methodist Episcopal Church. I'm the daughter of a long line of strong African American Christian women who made a way out of no way. And I'm reminded that for so many of us the very act of breathing is a subversive act, particularly as we think about this moment when we're battling a disease, an invisible enemy that is seeking to steal our breath.

Unfortunately, for some communities around the world, the experience of breath being stolen is not unfamiliar. I'm reminded of the last words of Eric Garner, "I can't breathe, I can't breathe." And for so many people whose lives have been pushed to the margins, the very act of breathing and saying, "I am here, I'm not going anywhere, I am rooting" is a radical act, and that is sacred. And so my call is to listen to the wisdom of the elders, of the church mothers and the senior saints, of those who have been around the block, who have seen the horrors of the world and lived to tell the tale. Because we are living, God willing, to tell the tale of this moment. And it is a beautiful thing to be able to breathe.

A Bridge Between Heaven and Earth

Kabir Helminski is a shaikh of the Mevlevi Order of Sufis, Rumi translator, and author of The Knowing Heart. *Camille Helminski is the author of* Women of Sufism: A Hidden Treasure, Writings and Stories of Mystic Poets, Scholars, and Saints. *She is cofounder with her husband of the Threshold Society.*

℘

My wife, Camille, and I are both connected with the tradition of Sufism and particularly the tradition of Jalāl ad-Dīn Rumi. In our understanding of this life, the human being is a bridge between heaven and earth. If we open up to the divine, we can bring divine qualities into the world. And this is done through what we call the spiritual heart, which is an organ of perception that can perceive the universe and life qualitatively. The heart knows relationship, the heart knows value, the heart knows truth. The heart is the true mind. The thinking mind is just a servant of the heart. It's in the heart that we can sense what is most valuable, and it's through the heart that we can find our connection to the divine. So let the heart be your center of gravity. Through your heart, you are the bridge between heaven and earth. I'll close with the words of Jalāl ad-Dīn Rumi, which we have translated. This is addressed to God.

> *The heart is your student,*
> *for love is the only way we learn.*
> *Night has no choice but to grab the feet of daylight.*
> *It's as if I see Your Face everywhere I turn.*
> *It's as if Love's radiant oil*
> *never stops searching*
> *for a lamp in which to burn.*

DIVAN-E SHAMS-E TABRIZI: QUATRAIN 353

One Million Arab Women

Sheikha Intisar Salem Al Ali Al Sabah is the founder and editorial director of Lulua Publishing. She is a member of the consultative board of the United Nations Development Program bureau in Kuwait and the founder of the Intisar Foundation, which provides support to women in war-torn environments.

ᴄ⁓

I started the Intisar Foundation to use drama therapy to psychologically support women affected by war. Why drama therapy? It's easy, it's engaging, it's gentle, it's nonstigmatizing, and it's powerful. It's psychology and theater combined. And because of this, women are growing their voices, growing their confidence, growing their self-worth. And with all this growth, they're becoming peacemakers in their families, in their communities, and in the region.

Our goal for the Arab world is to support one million Arab women peace agents. I would love for all of us to become peace agents, and learn to find peace in ourselves as our fears are coming up—to learn to voice them, talk about them, and hear what others have to say. That's what we do with our women every day. Through the expression of our fears, we feel our emotions, and then let them go—because only then can we have peace, and only then can our world be in peace.

Your Joy and Sorrow I Make It Mine

Roshi Joan Halifax is an author, teacher, anthropologist, socially engaged Buddhist, and abbot of Upaya Institute and Zen Center in Santa Fe, New Mexico.

⌒

This is a time to wake up. We have a chance to do something rare and essential, and that is to take the suffering of this situation and turn it toward the good.

I live in a monastery. I also live in the wider world, and part of that wider world includes populations of great vulnerability, whether we're talking about impoverished people living on the margins of our society in sacrifice zones, or people who are unsheltered, or people who cannot access adequate health care. And one of the things that we do in our monastery is to enact a ceremony called the Gate of Sweet Nectar that acknowledges the truth of suffering.

At the very beginning of the ceremony, we chant:

> *Calling out to hungry hearts, everywhere through endless time.*
> *You who wander, you who thirst, I offer you this bodhi mind.*
> *Calling out to hungry spirits, everywhere through endless time,*
> *Calling out to hungry hearts, all the lost and left behind.*
> *Gather around and share this meal, your joy and sorrow, I make*
> *it mine.*

At the end of every day that we practice at Upaya, we chant the Vows of the Bodhisattvas. The Bodhisattvas are those beings who are dedicated to ending the suffering of others. The vows are:

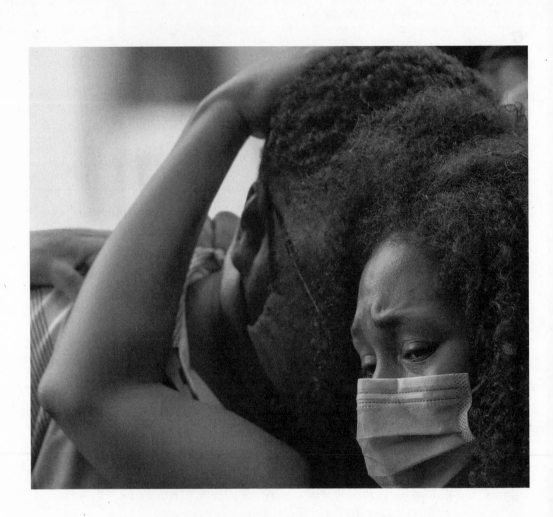

Jacob Blake, Sr., whose son was shot by police, is comforted by a family member at a press conference. Kenosha, WI, USA. August 2020.

Creations are numberless; I vow to free them.
Delusions are inexhaustible; I vow to transform them.
Reality is boundless; I vow to perceive it.
The awakened way is unsurpassable; I vow to embody it.

Let's meet this world with compassion, with sanity, and with a commitment to love and justice. Let's wake up. Let's live by vow. Let's be a Buddha now, a Bodhisattva now.

When One Tree Is Struggling

Christian Wiman is a poet and author of Survival Is a Style. *Krista Tippett is a Peabody Award–winning journalist,* New York Times–*bestselling author, and the founder of the On Being Project.*

ᢕ

KRISTA: My work is about pursuing the great questions of meaning and humanity: What does it mean to be human? How do we want to live? And I've started realizing in recent years that poetry is perhaps the best form for getting at these raw human realities, and not just the question of who we are, but who we want to be.

Christian Wiman is one of our great poets, and he wrote a book well before the pandemic, called *Survival Is a Style.* As I was reading the book, it felt prophetic to me. It's so vivid in these pages, Chris, that you have faced your mortality. This has been a defining thing for you, this diagnosis of cancer that came to you a long time ago and that you live with now. Your book made me think we all could face our mortality, but we don't. And yet now, through the pandemic, we are all conscious of our mortality in a new way, and all together at the same time. Our global experience has come closer to the personal experience you've been working through by way of poetry and theology.

CHRIS: I think that's true—some things actually don't seem to come into existence until we turn our attention to them, and poetry is especially good at focusing attention. I wanted to read one poem that is about turning your attention to something and feeling it come alive. It's called "When the Time's Toxins":

> When the time's toxins
> have seeped into every cell
> and like a salted plot
> from which all rain, all green, are gone
> I and life are leached
> of meaning
> somehow a seed
> of belief
> sprouts the instant
> I acknowledge it:
> little weedy hardy would-be
> greenness
> tugged upward
> by light
> while deep within

roots like talons
are taking hold again
of this our only earth.

KRISTA: What you just read is so visual and sensory that it unites our minds, our spirits, and our physical being. It lands in our bodies. It's all there in just a few lines.

CHRIS: That's the relief it gives me. It seems like difficulty but it's actually not so difficult. It's simply the words working together, like the Gerard Manley Hopkins poem that begins *"As kingfishers catch fire, dragonflies draw flame."* You don't have to worry about the meaning so much.

KRISTA: Bringing all those sounds together plants us in our wholeness.

CHRIS: Interesting you use the word *plant*. I listened to a sermon a couple of weeks ago by a friend of mine in Chicago. He mentioned that the roots underneath the trees communicate with each other and actually when one tree is struggling, the other trees will send extra nutrients to that tree. We can talk about the ways we're united, but we're united because the natural world is united. It's not something we're forcing into existence.

The World's Most Sensitive Cargo

Naomi Shihab Nye is a poet, songwriter, and novelist.

⁓

Feeling united with ourselves—that's the gift that poetry gives to listeners or to writers, and I think we're all people who have poetry channels inside our brains whether we identify as poets or not. I'd like to share a poem I wrote called "Shoulders."

Shoulders

A man crosses the street in rain,
stepping gently, looking two times north and south,
because his son is asleep on his shoulder.
No car must splash him.
No car drive too near to his shadow.
This man carries the world's most sensitive cargo
but he's not marked.
Nowhere does his jacket say FRAGILE,
HANDLE WITH CARE.
His ear fills up with breathing.
He hears the hum of a boy's dream
deep inside him.
We're not going to be able
to live in this world
if we're not willing to do what he's doing

with one another.

The road will only be wide.

The rain will never stop falling.

We are More Than What We See from Outside

Angélique Kidjo, called "Africa's premier diva" and "the Queen of African music," is an actress, an activist, and a four-time Grammy Award–winning singer-songwriter.

ᕔ

United we prevail. Divided we fail. All my life that has been my philosophy, to build bridges between people and between cultures, because we are all one. I was lucky to be raised by a large number of males and females in my village who I could run to and ask questions—and they always said to me, "As long as you love yourself, respect yourself, and give that respect and love to other people, a human being is not a matter of color. We are more than what we see from outside." That has been my call to unite from the moment I could think.

That's why I am so passionate about the youth of today. I'm working with the invisible ones, the poorest of the poorest in villages where there is barely electricity, and I helped the girls build a solar business. We changed our curriculum to make it business oriented, because that is what they asked for. They want to have a future, not just to be married young. Three years ago, they decided to produce and sell solid soap and liquid soap. They told me, "Soap is at the center of our hygiene, our livelihood and our life. When we go to the city to buy the soap, we come back and have to ration that soap. We wash ourselves, or we wash the dishes or we wash the clothes."

They began selling soap, and during the pandemic, they were ready. They became the agent of change in their communities. They immediately went from home to home to provide the soap for the elderly, the chief of village, the men and women, little kids. They went to the local radio and sent the message to people about soap and fighting the virus. That's why I say when you reach out to the youth in Africa, respecting them, listening to them, and reacting upon their needs, they become the agents of change, the ones who save lives, the ones who bring community together, the ones who provide for the elderly, for the middle class, and for the lowest class. They want to be part of something bigger, and make all of us part of it as well.

The Seven Fires Prophecy

Sachem Hawkstorm is the chief of the Schaghticoke First Nations people, an Indigenous rights activist, and an environmentalist.

ᯤ

In this time of confusion, I look to our teaching of the Seven Fires Prophecy—and all of the prophecies that are coming to fruition in these times. The Seven Fires Prophecy says that there will come a time when our elders will be asleep, when our youth will not have grown up in the traditional knowledge, and yet our youth will have to lead us in a choice between two paths.

One path is the scorched path—the path that's most traveled, the path of extractive industry, the path of the Industrial Revolution, the path that gives us everything our fast-paced lives demand. This is the path we're on now, with everything happening as soon as we want it.

The other is the green path. The green path is not so well traveled anymore. And it's a much harder path to take now, because we have to let go of some of the things we think we need. The computers, the phones, the cars, the way we're living, the things we're eating—all might have to shift if we are going to live in reciprocity and walk on the green path.

Yet the pandemic has forced us to see that we don't need as much as we thought we did.

We've been slowed down, put in our homes, sent to our rooms. And many of us are seeing that all the things we didn't have time to do before, now we have time for. All those things that we thought were so important, now maybe don't seem so important. All those things we thought it would destroy our lives not to have—maybe they're the wrong things.

We've learned from watching this disease that it doesn't recognize borders—just like our environment doesn't. If we do something in the US, it's going to affect Siberia. If we destroy the rain forest in Brazil, it's going to affect the Arctic. We're interconnected, not isolated. So we need to come together as a global community to fix the problems we created when we thought we were isolated. That's the real call to community. If we stop living beyond our means, and stop living for something else, and come back and slow down and live in right relationships with each other and the earth, we can walk on the green path. But we have to walk it together. For our actions to matter we have to take them together.

Hashim, a health-care worker, greets his daughter through a closed door. New Rochelle, NY, USA. April 2020.

No Boundaries Are Real

Deepak Chopra is a leading figure in the New Age movement, an advocate of alternative medicine, and bestselling author of books ranging from metaphysics to religious theory.

⤴

A new story is emerging for humanity—a story of justice and joy and happiness and health. But right now, we're going through a grieving process. We're asking, "Why me?" We're becoming angry and resentful. We're starting to feel helpless and resigned.

But at this point, something magical can happen: If we surrender to the grieving process, there is acceptance, and when there is acceptance, people find meaning. Today we can find meaning by getting over our lost story and inventing a new story, a new meaning, a new mind-set—because the pandemic has shown us what science has already told us: no boundaries are real.

Right now, we need to see this disruption not only as a death, but an opportunity for emergence. Social scientists say emergence happens when there is a shared vision, which we are embarking on now; when there is an amazing diversity of people who complement each other's strengths, and when these people create a community that can not only dream but can make the dream real by taking action. That is what we are doing. That is how we are creating a new story. And the mantra of the new story should be *love in action*.

Love without action is meaningless. Action without love is irrelevant. But when you have love in action, miracles happen. There's no other way. We cannot wait for governments. We cannot wait for businesses—because governments and businesses are a reflection of ourselves. They will change as we change.

Each of us, in this moment, needs to be a leader—a leader in our personal life, a leader in our families, a leader in our communities, a leader in our countries, a leader in our world. And leadership requires very few characteristics. Authenticity: Don't pretend to be who you're not. Integrity: Live up to your promises. And a higher calling: Take responsibility for our own well-being and the well-being of others also—even those who don't share our beliefs.

It starts with empathy, feeling what others feel. It moves to compassion, the desire to alleviate suffering. And once that happens, love emerges spontaneously as an expression of unity consciousness, not just the sentiment but the ultimate truth at the heart of creation.

That's the most important thing we can do—harness our love and compassion to promote well-being and ask each other "How can I help?" If we do that, we will move to the critical mass we need to create a new story.

V.

Our Only Chance
to Triumph

LOVE IN ACTION

Imam Omar Suleiman says no one should suffer alone. Killian Noe says we love people when their needs become real to us. Sarah B. says we need to be together, especially those of us who've been homeless. And Shaka Senghor asks us to see promise in the people in prison.

Imam Omar and Killian and Sarah and Shaka are speaking up for justice because they are close to people in need. Why does Shaka speak up for the incarcerated? Because he's been in prison with them. Why does Sarah care for the homeless? Because she's lived on the streets with them. But we can't leave the work of justice to the people who've suffered injustice. We have to cross boundaries.

Darius Baxter, who overcame the effects of violence and poverty after his

Monique Gray leads a chant at a Black Lives Matter protest. San Francisco, CA, USA. June 2020.

father was murdered, is now helping low-income families move into self-sufficiency. He says he's seeing people who in the past wouldn't be there for each other now standing up and supporting each other. How did this happen? People crossed a divide.

Crossing divides isn't easy, but it's necessary. Boundaries between people are barriers to justice. If we want change, we have to go places we've never gone and befriend people we've never known. We will demand justice when we are close to the people denied justice.

A call to justice is a call to unite.

A Revolution of Values

Shaka Sisulu Ndaba Mandela, and Biso Tutu-Gxashe are the grandsons of anti-apartheid leaders Walter Sisulu, Nelson Mandela, and Desmond Tutu. Martin Luther King III is the oldest living child of civil rights leader Martin Luther King Jr. Asha Ramgobin is the great-granddaughter of Mahatma Gandhi, leader of India's independence movement.

☙

SHAKA: As we go through this pandemic, I know we've all reflected on the values that strengthened our forefathers in their own times of uncertainty and isolation. I'm asking each of us to focus on a word that captures some of those values.

ASHA: The word that deeply motivated Gandhi is *love*. He said, "The sum total of the energy of mankind is not to bring us down but to lift us up—and that is the result of the definite, if unconscious, working of the law of love." Over time, Gandhi's idea of love expanded from the smaller to the wider to become a more all-encompassing notion that drove his search for God, truth, justice, and peace.

MARTIN: I would also say *love*. Dad had a sermon entitled "Levels of Love" and he went through all of them. The highest level of love is defined by the word *agape*, a love that is totally unselfish and seeks nothing in return. You love someone regardless of ethnicity, regardless of where they are on the planet. You love them because you know that the universal God loves you and calls you to do that. I believe that all the work that he and his team did with the modern civil rights movement was done out of love.

BISO: The word that comes to mind for me is *selflessness*. One of the things my grandfather always told me was that they made it through because they knew they were not alone.

NDABA: *Compassion*. When my grandfather was on Robben Island, he was able to teach himself how to become fluent in reading and writing Afrikaans. He said, "If you speak to a man in a language he understands, it will go to his head; if you speak to a man in language of his own, it will go to his heart." So they had to come up with the rule on Robben Island that no one can guard Mandela for more than three months, because he was able to touch them through language of their own, and through that bond he was able to smuggle in an extra couple of blankets or maybe at times a newspaper. When the authorities found this out, they were furious and had to switch the warden.

SHAKA: *Love* is the word that I had. Even though Walter Sisulu is well known for going to jail for nearly thirty years for his belief that South Africa should be a free nonracial country, he is also well known as one half of the love story between him and my grandmother, Albertina Sisulu. They shared a love that was crystallized by the hardships that his family endured. At one point in the struggle, my grandmother was one of the longest-banned people in the country, and my family had three generations in jail at the same time. Despite this, they stood together. My grandfather was one of the wisest and kindest, most loving men I've ever known.

Biso, as a man of the cloth, your grandfather always has had God to lean on, but what about your own challenges? Do you share the same faith?

BISO: I remember asking my grandfather, "When it was at its worst, how did you manage to stay strong and continue to fight for equal rights?" He told me two things. The first one I mentioned. He said, "Remember that we were not alone and that we were able to lean on each other for support." And the second, he said, "Those feelings of hurt and pain, it's okay to acknowledge those because we all hurt and suffer." Those are the things I remind myself of when I'm praying—that I'm not alone in this, that more people are going through the same thing.

SHAKA: Ndaba, what do you think your grandfather would be saying about the fear and isolation due to the pandemic? What would he be telling us to do?

NDABA: People are afraid. Their hopes are dwindling, especially those who are poor and don't have a job to provide food for their kids. I think Madiba would encourage us to keep the hope alive. We need to look at ourselves and draw the strength of our ancestors and our families to keep us standing strong in the face of this pandemic. We need unity.

SHAKA: Asha, how do we respond to this background of criticism that says maybe our agendas are just not radical enough?

ASHA: I don't think it's about not being radical enough. I certainly don't think that nonviolence was a mistake. Far from it. I think nonviolence is a radical stance and a principled approach. Right now, as consumers, as lawyers, as labor, noncooperation—saying no when we need to say no—is what we need to be doing more than ever before.

SHAKA: Martin, your father's struggles ranged from racial equality to economic equality. What do you think is the struggle in this era?

MARTIN: Some of it is still the same. Dad talked about eradicating the triple evils, which he defined as poverty, racism, and militarism. If we are looking from the perspective of COVID, the African American community in the United States and communities of color are still disproportionately affected. In Chicago, Detroit, and Milwaukee, the African American numbers of those who are dying is far higher than any other ethnic groups. So the biggest challenge is how do we create economic inclusion so that everyone benefits? Not everyone will be rich, but everyone should have a decent home. Should have decent education. Should have health care. Should have justice.

ASHA: Absolutely we need economic inclusion. Who do we really need to run a society? We need the nurses, we need the cleaners, we need grocery attendants. And yet these are the most underpaid, undervalued people in our community. We have experienced this form of economic exploitation for centuries now, and this coronavirus pandemic is showing us the fruit of it. Because while the virus attacks equally if it reaches you, the consequences affect you differently if you are Black or white, rich or poor.

SHAKA: Ndaba, what are your dreams for tomorrow's world?

NDABA: I want to see a world that stands up in the face of adversity, brother. I want to see a world that can come together and agree on certain moral principles. Once we agree on those moral principles, I believe there is no structure that can control us and make us do what we don't want to do. We need to seek the Nelson Mandela that exists in every one of us who will stand up for what is right, whether you have fear or not.

SHAKA: Martin, where do we go from here? Chaos or community?

MARTIN: There is an old saying that a politician thinks about the next election, but the statesperson plans for the next generation. We have to plan for generations yet unborn. If we want to create a world where everyone has a decent quality of life, has a home, has health care, has justice, has the freedom to choose, then we have to have community. Community is not easy to create, but it is in the depths of our souls. Dad called it a revolution of values. When we work in community, there is nothing on this planet that we cannot resolve. We have the capacity to be great, and it only takes a few good women and men to create that consciousness.

The Lowest Moment of Their Lives

David Brooks is a New York Times *columnist and the founder of Weave: The Social Fabric Project. Darius Baxter is a cofounder of UNITE and the founder of GOODProjects in Washington, DC. Sarah Hemminger is a social entrepreneur, scientist, and founder of Thread, an organization that connects high schoolers with supportive Johns Hopkins students.*

ᢕ

DAVID: I work at Weave: The Social Fabric Project. Weave supports organizations that offer a loving hand and an outstretched arm. Some feed the hungry, some care for the young, some bring neighborhoods together to solve problems, but all of them are about building community and connection. I found that many weavers took the lowest moment of their lives and made it the *defining* moment of their lives. They often had something bad happen to them. They lost a child, they went to prison, they were homeless, they saw their neighborhood crumbling around them, and in their moment of crisis, they found their purpose. They said, "I will work so other people don't have to suffer the way I have."

Their example showed me that when you're going through hard times you can either be broken or broken open. Some people shrivel and get hard and selfish. Some people become softer and more generous. They find depths inside that are often more beautiful than the surface, and in those depths is our unbelievable ability to care for one another.

People who have touched those deep spots have unleashed an energy, and they respond by building something so they can bring their gifts to the world. I'd like to introduce two people, friends of mine who have been building community for a long time: Darius Baxter of GOODProjects and Sarah Hemminger of Thread.

DARIUS: Your words are poignant, David, especially at this moment. I've had the blessed opportunity over the last four years to help stand up this amazing organization in DC with two of my lifelong friends, Danny Wright and Troye Bullock. When we started, our focus was to try to solve every problem that ever existed for any population here in DC: gun violence, homelessness, poor education systems. We were young and ambitious. I like to think we still are. But we quickly realized that in order to have the greatest level of impact, which is generational impact, we needed to focus our efforts and resources on supporting one community at a time. So, over the last two years in partnership with our funders at the Ford Foundation and other institutions, we're helping to move five hundred families in southwest Washington, DC, out of poverty and into fully realizing the American Dream.

Right now, the need is even more intense than when we started, and it's everywhere. Whether you're in southwest Washington, or in Ghana, or the south of France, there are families finding themselves at the lowest points they've ever been. And you're also seeing people who wouldn't typically be there for one another standing up, joining hands, and supporting each other.

So, I want us to be able to look at this moment and ask ourselves: What are we doing right? This is the Great Reset for our time, no matter how rich or poor, everyone is at home. It's the great equalizer for a lot of us. We're realizing the humanity in every single person. We need to take the lessons we're learning in this moment and use them as the world begins to speed back up—so we can fight together against the pressures of capitalism, of bigotry, of divisiveness. There's a lot of positives in the negatives, and if we can teach ourselves and our children the lessons of this moment, we'll be a better species in the long run.

SARAH: I agree with Darius, a lot more people are suffering and a lot more people are supporting each other. The young people I work with at Thread are faced with significant achievement and opportunity gaps. COVID-19 has just exacerbated that, from food insecurity, to unequal education, to health disparities. As the pandemic took hold, we called all our young people, and we started hearing stories of kids taking multiple bus rides to get a meal. So we mobilized our community and made sure that all of our young people and their families had weeks of groceries in their pantries. And then we realized we needed a more scalable and efficient solution. So we leveraged the sixteen years of good relationships in the community to partner with New Psalmist

Baptist Church and local nonprofits to purchase large quantities of food from local distributors that would normally go to restaurants. We've now served over fifteen hundred families, and we just launched a project with a dozen different partners, called Food with a Focus, to help feed more families across Baltimore.

In the middle of all this, I received a text from a student alum of ours, Leroy, with a note and a picture of a gift that Thread had given him a decade ago at his high school graduation. It was a picture frame that had the word *resilient* written in it, a word that his Thread family had chosen as a reflection of what he brought into our lives. He saw the frame as a reminder that he was resilient enough to make it through this. What I don't think he understood is that the fact that he had kept the frame for a decade and took the time to reach out and make sure I was okay gave *me* resilience. It was exactly what I needed to get by.

Thread is not a group of haves helping a group of have-nots. We're a family leaning on each other. I want us to continue to see all individuals as human beings with value. I want us to continue to champion frontline health-care workers and grocery-store workers, and I want us to be able to give people food without judgment. If we can get to a place of vulnerability where we can accept help from others, and then offer it back to them when they need it, we can build a society that helps everyone thrive.

@blackfairygodmother

Elizabeth Gilbert is the New York Times*–bestselling author of*
Eat, Pray, Love *and* City of Girls.

∽

There is a woman whose work I have admired for a very long time, long before the coronavirus disaster hit. Her name is Simone Gordon. She's an activist—an extraordinary, generous, powerful force in her community, which is Newark, New Jersey. She's an African American woman who goes by the social media handle @blackfairygodmother. She was formerly homeless; a survivor of domestic violence; the mother of an autistic, nonverbal child; and she is also putting herself through nursing school because she wants to serve humanity even more. As if that were not enough, what she does in her free time—although I don't know how she *has* free time—is she runs on social media these small, direct fundraisers for other women of color who are in need. She was doing this long before the coronavirus hit. It's like she was building the ark before the flood, taking care of her community in this intimate, passionate way.

I've learned from following Simone that sometimes the difference between a mother and her children staying in their home or being evicted is two hundred dollars. The difference between keeping the lights on and losing power may be seventy-five dollars. These relatively small, in many cases heartbreakingly small, amounts of money can mean the difference between saving somebody's life or destroying it. For instance, two hundred dollars in groceries might make it so that a mom doesn't have to choose between feeding her kids or fixing the car she needs to get to her job. I've been supporting Simone for years, but now that the coronavirus has hit, I'm getting my community on social media—which is largely made up of white, progressive women—to help Simone and her community. I feel like that's the least we can do for a community that has, because of traditional racism and injustice in this country, suffered and struggled for so long and did not need this disaster on top of everything else.

Every chance that I get, I direct the followers of my work to follow Simone's work so that we can join together and move resources to hardworking people whose work has been holding up the economy of this country for a very long time. If you would like to be part of that, you can follow Simone. A little bit of money chipped in from a large community over time can help a community that needed help long before this, needs help now, and will likely still be needing love and support long after this virus is over.

My prayer is that once this crisis has passed, we can start talking about why there are such enormous disparities in income and in racial justice in this country. But for now, I would just say follow Simone's work. Helping her makes me feel like I'm not helpless—that there is always something I can do to be of service.

Our Only Chance to Triumph

Sister Norma Pimentel is a member of the Missionaries of Jesus, and has dedicated her life to caring for migrants on both sides of the U.S.-Mexico border.

ᢅᢇ

In these times, we are more aware of how fragile and vulnerable we each are, no matter who we are. Our only chance to triumph is to help each other, excluding no one. Call your church. I'm sure they're doing something. Please reach out to those who are trying to help the families.

What Service Is

Meisha Lerato Robinson, a cofounder of UNITE and former corporate brand manager, served in the Peace Corps in Benin and South Africa and is the founder of I Am, We Are, a youth empowerment initiative anchored in South Africa and dedicated to building a world where all youth are socially engaged, globally aware, and economically free.

⁓

My mother used to tell me that to whom much is given, much is expected. I have taken that to heart. I feel all the gifts we have been given in life—our time, our talent, or our treasure—God gave them to us so that we would give them to others, give them to the people we meet throughout our day, give them to the people in our community and in our home. That is what service is.

When Their Needs Become Real to Us

Killian Noe is the founder of Recovery Café, a refuge for Seattle residents experiencing homelessness and mental health challenges. Tiffany T. came to Recovery Café seeking support for a drinking issue ten years ago, and today serves as its operations manager. Joan P. and Sara B. are members.

⁓

KILLIAN: There is a oneness in the human family that we deny at our peril. And this crisis has exposed the cruel inequality in our systems and our society,

*Dominick Walton, who is herself experiencing homelessness,
distributes food to others. Houston, TX, USA. April 2020.*

but it's also revealed the love and the power of relationships. We don't love in the abstract. We love people when their needs become real to us. We need to let our hearts break. And if we let our hearts break over the inequality and the suffering of people who have been left out for a long time, we can choose to live like we really belong to each other.

JOAN P.: I run into people who are despairing, and I say to them, "The world is a better place with you in it."

TIFFANY T.: I just had a recent loss with my mother, and I think pain can change things. Pain can bring the love. Whenever you're in pain and you're able to love others and reach out, that is what changes the game. That is how you heal.

SARA B.: We need to be together, especially people coming from the same kind of history that I've experienced: homelessness, mental health issues, addiction issues. So, don't be afraid to ask for help. There's no shame in asking for help.

Change from Being a Spectator to a Player

Chris Paul is point guard for the Oklahoma City Thunder, president of the Nation Basketball Players Association, and founder of the Chris Paul Family Foundation. Konrad Lyle and Corinne Nevinny are cofounders of Radical Relief Fund. Corinne is also cofounder and managing partner at Avestria Ventures, a venture capital fund focusing on women's health and women in life sciences.

⌒

KONRAD LYLE: We've been doing research on how to make an impact with our giving, and we're convinced that the best approach for us right now is to give directly to households that are in need. That sends a message to people that "you are part of a community that cares about you and supports you." That's a radical idea.

CORINNE NEVINNY: There is a big imbalance today between the people who have deep resources and the people who have big needs, and the people with resources should be giving more. We need to motivate each other. My mother always used to say, "If I could, I would. If you can, you should." That message never gets softer for me; it gets louder.

CHRIS PAUL: I believe most people want to make a difference, but they don't always know how. When people come to me for advice on giving, I always say that the most valuable thing we have is our time—including the time to get

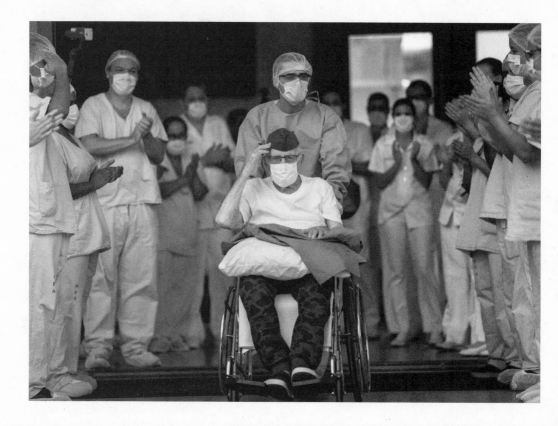

World War II combat veteran Ermando Armelino, 99,
salutes the health-care workers who helped him recover from
COVID-19. Brasília, Brazil. April 2020.

together to talk about taking action. I've seen so many different people come together lately who in other times never would have met with each other, and one person says, "Let's do this," and everyone joins in. I think that power of connection is starting to show its face, and connection leads to action.

Some people still hold back because they feel their part won't make any difference. They tell me, "Man, I can't help all these different people." But that's not how to look at it. I tell them, "Anything is something." If you can help just one person, one family, you got to do it. Then you've made the biggest change possible—the change from being a spectator to a player.

A Duty to Serve

John Bridgeland, a cofounder of UNITE, served as director of the White House Domestic Policy Council under President George W. Bush. He is the vice chair of Malaria No More, an organization working to end malaria in sub-Saharan Africa.

ervice transforms us. When you serve a great cause, as we see the nurses and doctors and health-care workers doing today, you lose yourself and find a greater purpose. The pursuit of Happiness—with a capital *H* from the Declaration of Independence—is not about just individual happiness—a car, or a home, or even protecting your family; it is a cooperative enterprise we help one another achieve. We have to rescue that notion back, particularly in these times of crisis and vulnerability, and recognize that we have a duty to serve one another, and only through that service can we find our own happiness and heal our nation.

Please Go to Tibet

Arlene Samen is a nurse practitioner in maternal fetal medicine and founder of One Heart Worldwide Foundation, an organization dedicated to saving the lives of women and children in childbirth.

 ҉

Twenty-three years ago, I met His Holiness the Dalai Lama, and he said, "Will you please go to Tibet and help the women and children who die in childbirth?" My own mother had lost several children, so I left my job at the University of Utah and spent the next ten years working in Tibet, building the first maternal and child health project and reducing maternal mortality from one in a hundred mothers to zero. After some changes happened in China, we had to leave and we started working in Nepal, where we have been for the last ten years. We have built 483 birthing centers. We have trained thousands of health-care workers, and maternal mortality is significantly dropping there because access to care saves lives.

And we are now working hard to help mothers bring their babies safely into the world in a time of COVID.

Never Returning to
the Classroom

Julia Roberts is an Academy Award–winning actress and producer.

༄

Recently, I traveled to Vietnam and met inspiring young women who had overcome unimaginable obstacles to their education, including extreme poverty and gender discrimination. With the support of a nonprofit called Room to Read, they successfully charted their own paths and became the heroes of their own stories, going on to university, pursuing careers, and starting small businesses.

With schools closed because of COVID in countries where gender inequality is prevalent, girls are at acute risk of never returning to the classroom. It's crucial that we do what we can to ensure education endures for young women in the most vulnerable communities.

Small Gestures Can Make
a Big Difference

Jennifer Garner is an actress, producer, and early-childhood education activist. Mark Shriver is senior vice president of U.S. Programs & Advocacy for Save the Children.

ᴄᴏ

JENNIFER: Every month for years, I've been reading to students at Pleasant Hill Elementary, one of my favorite schools in all West Virginia, my home state. I've read to them over Skype from movie sets and my living room and my kitchen and in my pajamas. And I've definitely kept up with it during the lockdown.

MARK: Jen, we've been together at Save the Children for a dozen years now. Tell us why you love reading to kids so much.

JENNIFER: We get to visit kids all across the country growing up in rural poverty, and see the amazing work that can happen from giving a child a little bit of help, some fun, some connection with their mom. But I felt kind of removed from it, and I wanted to have more contact with the kids, so reading was a way to do one small thing that was just mine.

MARK: I heard you say "some connection with their mom." You have a great connection with your parents, right? And your mom was the first generation to go to college.

JENNIFER: Both my parents. And one of the things that I hold so dear in my relationship with my mom is that she read to me every night all the way through middle school. She would stay up and we would read *Anne of Green Gables* or we'd read plays. And she made that time for me with everything else she had to do. Now, because of working with you, I've been talking to parents about the fun and joy you can give your kid by reading to them.

There are so many different ways to be helpful. You don't have to be fancy. My mom goes to a kindergarten out in the middle of West Virginia and reads every month as well. She shows up and takes a couple of books. I'm sending her books all the time. People should go find a local school or a kid or even a senior citizen to read to. They'll love it.

MARK: Small gestures can make a big difference. Do you ever get discouraged when you meet with families and kids who are struggling during this pandemic?

JENNIFER: I get discouraged when you and I are somewhere, and I feel like people aren't listening. But when I go and meet the moms and the kids and I see the difference that the people with Save the Children are making in their lives, that gives me energy.

MARK: And you just keep that energy up, despite getting knocked back or getting turned down.

JENNIFER: I do if you do! Any time my energy lags, you say, "*Come on!*" We've done that for each other for a long time.

MARK: I keep going back to the Teddy Roosevelt quote about the credit belongs to the person in the arena who's trying day in and day out. Bishop Jakes talks about putting faith in the driver's seat and fear in the backseat. When I see those kids doing the chicken dance with you and hitting the dab, that's such positive energy. Despite the fact there's so much pain in the world, I just want to thank you so much, Jennifer, for giving us that energy and spreading that love.

JENNIFER: Thank you, Mark, for the partnership and the platform. We have a lot more work to do. So, every single day, faith in the driver's seat.

MARK: Faith in the driver's seat, fear in the back. Small gestures, big difference.

They Risk Getting Arrested

Laurene Powell Jobs is the founder of Emerson Collective, a social change organization that advocates for educational reform, health-care access, immigrant rights, and environmental conservation.

☙

This crisis has laid bare a cruel truth. Our societies have created all kinds of divisions. In America, the pandemic has exacerbated long-standing inequities. One of the most profound inequities is our treatment of eleven million undocumented immigrants, many of whom are serving on the front lines of our country's response to the virus. They're caring for the sick in our hospitals. They're growing food in our fields and delivering it to our homes.

They are in so many ways doing the work that's been deemed essential to the functioning of our economy and our society, and they're doing it at great risk to their own health and the health of their loved ones. But unlike others, they can't get support from the government. They can't get economic relief if they get laid off. They can't get medical care if they get sick. If they come forward for a test, they risk getting arrested. Why can't we see that denying rights to this community risks the health and well-being of all of us? This is a moment for us to shed false barriers and face this crisis together.

A Metro bus driver pausing while on break.
Los Angeles, CA, USA. April 2020.

Put Them in the Front

Dr. Antonia Novello served as the fourteenth United States Surgeon General from 1990 to 1993. She was the first woman and first Hispanic to hold the position.

~

I've been dealing with the COVID-19 pandemic at all levels, from the beginning until today. It's important in moments like this to know that we are not alone, we are not an island, and we are all interdependent in everything we do. We're in the middle of a pandemic that we never wanted or expected. But I have to tell you: we have become so resilient. We are learning that we need the information and the supplies, but that's not enough unless we work to make each other's lives better. We must never split ourselves between races or between genders or between religions. We're all one, and this pandemic has put it in the biggest perspective of all: alone we cannot survive.

This is why it's crucial that when this is over, we recognize the heroes of the pandemic. There have been plenty, the first responders, the minorities who have been infected more than the rest just because of the jobs they hold. They are the ones who brought you food, they are the ones in construction, they are the ones in hospitality, they are the ones in transportation, they are the ones in health care, they are the ones in the uniformed services, they are the ones who sweep your streets and collect your garbage. They are the ones we will be honoring when we are done with this pandemic. When the moment comes and we clap for the heroes, don't forget that sometimes the biggest heroes are in the back, and the time has come to put them in the front.

Already Pushed to the Margins

Dr. Uché Blackstock is an emergency medicine physician based in New York City and the founder and CEO of Advancing Health Equity, an organization dedicated to addressing racialized health disparities. Dr. Ashwin Vasan is president and CEO of Fountain House, a national nonprofit organization that serves people living with mental health issues.

∽

UCHÉ: Over the last few weeks, I've been seeing patients on the front lines and it's been very scary, to be honest. I've never seen anything like it in fifteen years of practice. We've also noticed in New York City that our black and brown communities have been most heavily affected by COVID-19. We hope that, now that these inequities have been exposed, we can address them. Dr. Vasan, you also do health equity work. Can you tell me what you're seeing?

ASHWIN: I'm seeing on both fronts, whether it's in my clinical role or in my role at Fountain House, that the impact of this pandemic is falling disproportionately on already vulnerable communities, and that includes not only racial and socioeconomic disparities that you highlighted, but also disparities based on other forms of marginalization—whether it's people who are chronically homeless, people who are incarcerated or formerly incarcerated, and people living with preexisting mental illness. The other thing I'm seeing is a coming wave, a second pandemic, as some are calling it, of mental health concerns. I think that's simply a function of the conditions and the stress we're living in. If you're already vulnerable, that's just a recipe for more challenges. We can see this wave coming, and we're going to have to address it.

UCHÉ: As you know, both in the short and long term, we need to focus on the social determinants of health, like quality education, adequate housing, and gainful employment, so we can ensure these communities are no longer so vulnerable.

ASHWIN: I completely agree. You and I, Uché, are experiencing the same thing—which is isolation, the inability to be close to our friends, to our colleagues, to people we love and care about—and we see the effect that is having on our own well-being, our health, our sense of self, our sense of purpose. Now imagine the same set of feelings felt by people who are already pushed to the margins, already socially isolated, already at risk of "falling through the cracks" of some of our systems.

I hope this is a moment when we can spare time and concern for someone who's going through the same thing as we are, just in a more extreme form. This is one of the few times in living memory when we're all experiencing some approximation of the same conditions, and then of course it's disproportionately more extreme for people who are already vulnerable. So this is an opportunity for us to connect across income, class, race, socioeconomic status—all the social determinants of health—and work for those on the other end of the spectrum from us.

Not That Strong by Ourselves

Simon Sinek is a motivational speaker and the author of five books, including Start with Why *and* The Infinite Game.

༄

H uman beings are not that strong by ourselves. We cannot lift heavy weights by ourselves and we cannot solve complex problems by ourselves. But in groups, surrounded by people who share our values and beliefs, we are remarkable.

Well, we all need more help now than ever before, *and* this is also the first time in my lifetime we can relate to somebody on the other side of the planet, people who are different from us, people we will never probably have a chance to meet. Because of COVID-19, there is a shared human experience that almost everyone in the world can relate to. And few things bring people together more than shared hardship and shared experience.

Compassionate Release

Van Jones is a CNN political contributor, host of The Van Jones Show *and* The Redemption Project, *which advocates for individuals in the criminal justice system. Phil Bryant served as governor of Mississippi from 2012 to 2020.*

༄

VAN: A plague like this goes from body to body with no respect for ideology or race or nationality. Our movement has to go from heart to heart with the same speed and power. As a strong Democrat, I'm proud to have worked with this strong Republican governor Phil Bryant for many years to help people behind bars. I'm sad to say in the US we have the world's largest prison population. Those people are in harm's way with this virus, and we cannot forget about them. The virus moves five to fifteen times faster through a prison population than through a normal population. We hope that governors and sheriffs and others will use compassionate release to let the older and sicker ones go to home confinement safely and let them survive. No one was condemned to die by a virus, no matter what they did.

The Reform Alliance, which I'm a part of, has gotten about 250,000 masks into jails and prisons, and has worked closely with the White House, with twenty-six governors, and with the Correctional Leaders Association to help people behind bars get safely home. About 30,000 people have come home so far. We need more to come home. This is about taking a strong stand for "the least of these" in this time of trouble, including those in prison. I know Governor Bryant feels the same way.

PHIL: People say to me, "How in the world did you and Van Jones come together?" We came together over a common belief that there are those in prison who need to be there, and there are those there who maybe we're just mad at. But as we see this pandemic going into the correctional facilities, we have a responsibility to keep it from spreading. Can we sanitize the conditions there and protect those inmates? Many of these people are our fathers, our friends, our wives, our loved ones who made a mistake, got caught in the trap of addiction, and are in prison now. We need to help them.

Mississippi began criminal justice reform in 2014. We followed that with working with the president of the United States on the First Step Act. I joined the president and Kim Kardashian for an event at the White House, and it was filled with people who were united behind criminal justice reform. It's time for us to bring that feeling back across this nation, not to criticize, not to judge anyone, but to lift everyone up and help one another.

VAN: I want to say a prayer for the people who are living behind bars and the people working behind bars, the guards, correctional officers, food services people. They go in and out of those prisons. You cannot defeat a plague on the outside of a prison if you don't defeat it on the inside, because those doors open and close every day. I stand with Governor Phil Bryant to say this is not about race or ideology. It's about human beings. We're all children of the same creator and we all deserve the same care. And I want to call on anyone with the power to give compassionate release to the old, to the sick, to the people who can come home safely—please use your power for good.

In a Six-by-Nine Cell

Shaka Senghor is the author of Writing My Wrongs: Life, Death, and Redemption in an American Prison, *a bestselling memoir of his nineteen years in prison, including seven years spent in solitary confinement.*

ᗢ

I grew up in Detroit. Got caught up in the streets when I was fourteen. When I was seventeen, I was shot. At nineteen, I shot and tragically caused a man's death, which led to me being sentenced to seventeen to forty years in prison. I ended up serving a total of nineteen of that. Seven of those years was in solitary. That is twenty-three-hour-a-day lockdown, in a six-by-nine cell.

When I was first in solitary, I remember feeling a high level of anxiety—kind of like what we're experiencing now in quarantine during this epidemic, where we feel boxed in, we feel isolated, we feel like there is no end to this thing. That's what was happening for me inside prison. It was the darkest time of my life, but it was in that space that I actually found my deeper life. That's when I began this journey of transformation.

I was fortunate to be literate and to have great mentors who guided me to amazing books that helped me understand the practice of meditation, and journaling, and transformative honesty about the decisions I've made and the things that happened in my life—and centering myself in the moment as opposed to focusing on the past or the future.

And what I learned is that I can only control myself, my thoughts, my feelings—and that if I can get through the pain of each moment, I can come out on the other side a better person. But in order to do that, I had to give myself the grace to say, "Hey, this doesn't feel good today." And by doing that, I was able to see myself through a very difficult time.

I believe that's the call for all of us today. If you give yourself just a little bit of grace, it will allow you to come out on the other side as a different human being. This is important because now there are 2.5 million men and women incarcerated in America. America houses 25 percent of the world's population of incarcerated people, even though we make up only 5 percent of the world population.

So I ask you to think about people in those situations who are vulnerable and who are suffering. We can collectively make a difference. But it starts with us having the ability to say we don't feel great today, but there is a brighter tomorrow, and that requires a little bit of grace and a lot of love and compassion and empathy not only for ourselves, but for others.

So this is a call for us to think the best of our fellow human beings despite their circumstances, and believe that they can add meaning and value to society when they are supported with the resources, compassion, and empathy that allow them to show up in the world as the best version of themselves.

None of Us Will Suffer Alone

Imam Omar Suleiman is an author, civil rights activist, professor, and founder and president of the Yaqeen Institute for Islamic Research.

A few years after Katrina devastated New Orleans, on the tenth anniversary of another horrible tragedy that struck our nation, 9/11, the faith communities in our city decided to get together and do something that would symbolize our unity—something that would honor the memory of the devastation that New Orleans had faced and the devastation that we had faced together as a country.

So Jews, Christians, and Muslims formed a base of more than a thousand volunteers, and we headed to River Town, New Orleans, where we restriped the roads, redid the gardens, repainted the buildings, and restored the area in a way that no one had imagined possible. That night, we gathered in the mosque along with city officials and members of the broader community, and to symbolize our togetherness with a New Orleans twist, we had gumbo. But it wasn't just any gumbo; it was kosher and halal gumbo side by side. I'm not

Nursing home resident Albert Letellier, 86, grasps the hand of the director of the residence through a protective plastic sheet. Péruwelz, Belgium. July 2020.

going to say which gumbo was better, but it was a beautiful moment that many of us relished. And we recognized that if Hurricane Katrina had not devastated our city, perhaps we would not have tasted the sweetness of the unity we were tasting that evening.

Here we are almost fifteen years after Katrina, facing a different type of tragedy. During this crisis, many Americans will be driven to soup kitchens for the very first time in their lives. Many Americans will go to homeless shelters for the very first time in their lives.

This creates an opportunity for all of us—because when we heal one another, then God heals us. The Prophet Mohammed, peace be upon him, said, "Show mercy to those on the earth, and the one in the heavens will show mercy to you." He said, "No one of you believes until he loves for his brother what he loves for himself." And he said, "He is not a believer who sleeps with a stomach full while his neighbor is hungry."

All of us are experiencing some sort of vulnerability right now, but there are those who have been experiencing vulnerability for a long time, and their vulnerability has been compounded by this crisis. Perhaps, through empathy and through service, we can come together and care for one another—not out of a desire to get back to the old normal, but out of a desire to fulfill the dream of a united people who love one another, who care for one another, and who commit to one another that while every one of us may suffer, none of us will suffer alone.

VI.

Renew the Face
of the Earth

A CALL TO LOVE

When we're in a crisis, we tend to search for a new way, often revisiting lessons we ignored when things were going well. And the greatest of these lessons is love.

Scarlett Lewis—whose six-year-old son Jesse was murdered at Sandy Hook Elementary School—opens part VI by urging us to "choose love." Ecumenical Patriarch Bartholomew says we must seek a new heaven and a new earth where all of creation is treated with love.

Reverend Dr. Jacqui Lewis says love is where God is, and God is where love is. Pastor Judah Smith says "when their story becomes our story," that is love. Rapper Common reads us a poem he wrote about love. Arthur Brooks says if you have fear, you need more love.

Demonstrators hug during a march for racial justice.
Los Angeles, CA, USA. June 2020.

Love is something we often ration. We reserve it for friends and family and people who love us back. But if we love those who love us and hate those who hate us, we stay stuck where we are.

Just as a tree takes in carbon and puts out oxygen to save the earth, we can take in hatred and give out love to save humanity. This is the defining spiritual gift. We all have it in some degree. We all can learn how to be wounded and treat others well—at least a little. And though many people seek innovations that will change the world, this is the innovation that will change *us*—answering ill will with good will, absorbing pain without passing it on. All our inventing and discovering and experimenting and exploring have led us back to this: The greatest human achievement is the power to love. No matter what.

Choose Love

Scarlett Lewis founded the Jesse Lewis Choose Love Movement in honor of her six-year-old son, who was killed in a shooting at Sandy Hook Elementary School in 2012.

༓

My six-year-old son, Jesse Lewis, was murdered in his first-grade classroom at Sandy Hook Elementary School alongside nineteen of his classmates and six educators in one of the worst mass murders in US history.

I didn't know how I was going to move forward. Then I found a message Jesse had written on our kitchen chalkboard shortly before he died. He wrote, "nurturing, healing love." Those words aren't something a first-grader would normally say, but they're in the definition of compassion across all cultures. I knew it was a message of comfort for his family and friends but also a directive. It was where we needed to turn in order to survive and thrive.

We can't always choose what happens to us, but we can always choose how we respond, and we can always respond with love. Nurturing, healing love actually translates into a powerful and profound formula that can lead us to choose love in any situation. I use it every day of my life to choose love over fear, and I want to share it with you.

It starts with courage. My son, Jesse, is known for saving nine of his first-grade classmates before losing his own life that day. He's actually on a short list for the Presidential Medal of Freedom for his final act of bravery. We all have the capacity for the courage Jesse showed. Scientific research says that courage is like a muscle, which means we can practice our courage and get stronger.

There's a lot of loss right now. But we can only focus on one thought at a time. We can either focus on the angry or fearful thought, or have the courage to choose a grateful one. There's always something to be grateful for. And it's not happiness that makes us grateful; it's gratefulness that makes us happy.

We also need to forgive. Forgiveness is the key to healthy relationships, and healthy relationships are the key to happiness. Forgiveness has been so healing for me. It gave me control of my thoughts. It helped me choose love over fear. Science tells us that the nurturing, healing love we give out we get back. When others see us doing something kind, they want to do something kind as well. When we practice compassion, we create a ripple effect that can circle the globe.

Love All of Creation

Ecumenical Patriarch of Constantinople Bartholomew I has served as head of the Eastern Orthodox Church since 1991.

⟶

Every day here at the Ecumenical Patriarchate, the sacred spiritual center of the Orthodox Church, we pray for the unity of all and for the peace of the whole world. The same words resonate each Sunday in every Orthodox Christian church all over the globe. Deep faith offers a profound vision of courage, consolation, and compassion. It suggests a new way of living and a new vision for the world.

We speak of this time of suffering as a crisis. But crisis in Greek, *κρίσις*, means judgment. We will be judged by the lessons we learn and by the changes we make in our lives and in our world.

We have seen how God's creation is larger than our concerns and interests. Larger than our communities and countries. Larger than any church or religion. We have been reminded of what the Sacred Scriptures teach, that we must love our neighbor, that we must love all of creation. We cannot take even the simplest things for granted. Every person, every relationship, every moment and every last detail in this life is a unique gift from God.

When the cloud of this crisis disappears, we should aspire to a new heaven and new earth, a world where poverty and hunger are eradicated, where understanding and tolerance are encouraged, and where all of creation is treated with love and respect. That is our prayer for everyone, and it is our prayer for all of you.

*A garbage collector works a fourteen-hour shift at
a landfill. Mexico City, Mexico. July 2020.*

The Essential Dignity of
Every Person's Life

*Bill Clinton served as president of the United States from
1993 to 2001.*

༄

In President Roosevelt's first inaugural address, which he gave in the teeth
of the Great Depression in America, he said, "We are aware now as we
have never been before of our interdependence." That simply means that we
need each other and we do better when we work together.

That has never been more clear to me as I have seen the courage and dignity of the first responders, the health-care workers, all the people who are
helping now to provide our food, our transportation, our basic services—each
of them in their own way taking some measure of personal risk to preserve
the essentials of a decent society as we try to overcome this epidemic. The
same, no doubt, has been true in nation after nation.

I am grateful for the people who are doing their part for those who would
otherwise be left behind. We have so much to do. But we know this. With all
the agony and all the loss, the essential dignity of every person's life has been
affirmed by those who are risking theirs to help the rest of us. The essential
dignity of a good society has been affirmed by those who have been good
citizens, practicing social distancing and doing other things to minimize the
chance that they or others will be infected.

The best thing we can do to honor those we have lost—and to save more
lives today and tomorrow—is to remember that we live in an interdependent
world. Our common humanity makes our interesting differences possible—

but our interesting differences can never justify denying our common humanity. This is what a call to unite ultimately means: Everyone counts. Everyone has a role to play. And we all do better when we help each other.

Countless Heroic Strangers

Martin Sheen is an Emmy Award–winning actor, director, and peace activist.

つ～

Ｔhis pandemic has made it quite clear that we are all responsible for each other and the world, which is exactly the way it is because, consciously or unconsciously, we have made it so. And while none of us made any of the rules that govern the universe, we do make *all* the rules that govern our own hearts and minds. We are all beneficiaries of those countless heroic strangers from every nation on earth who hasten to reassure us over and over again that the world is still a wonderful place despite our fear. And we are not asked to do great things. We are asked to do all things with greater care for the earth and for the very least among us.

This heroism takes our breath away, and it renews the face of the earth. But more importantly, it inspires us to help lift up the world and all its people to that place where the heart is without fear and the head is held high, where knowledge is free, where the world has not been broken up into fragments by narrow domestic walls, where words come out from the depths of truth and tireless striving stretches its arms toward perfection, where the clear stream of reason has not lost its way in the dreary desert sands of dead habit, where the

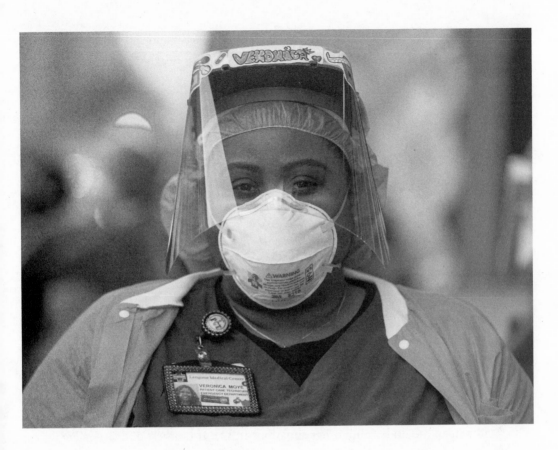

A patient-care technician outside NYU Langone Medical Center. New York, NY, USA. April 2020.

mind is led forward by Thee into ever-widening thought and action and into that heaven of freedom. Dear Father, let every country awake. Amen.

From the Same Womb

Cardinal Peter Turkson, former archbishop of Cape Coast, served as relator during the Second Special Assembly for Africa of the Synod of Bishops in 2009 and was president of the former Pontifical Council for Justice and Peace. He has been appointed by Pope Francis as first prefect of the new Dicastery for Promoting Integral Human Development, which provides aid to migrants and other victims of global conflict.

⁓

When I was a young lad growing up and studying classical languages, I learned that, in Greek, the words for brother and sister meant, etymologically, "from the same womb." This expression has stayed with me and helped me understand other situations in life. If brothers and sisters are united by the fact they are from the same womb—united in dignity, united in honor, united in rights, while maintaining differences in attitudes and habits—then the rest of the human race in a way is like that.

We are all, biblically at least, considered to be from the same origin, from the same father, but I'm from Africa, and many are from Europe and many are from China, and you can see our differences. If we are so different, can we still talk about being one? Yes, we can. The womb that makes us all one can be the womb of our parents, but it is also the womb of modern Earth, the planet that feeds us. We are one because we share a common womb of world culture, which determines what we study and what we pay attention to and how our lives are guided. We share a common womb of history, with all the world wars and everything that has happened that has brought us to this point. And lately, these days, we share the common womb of a pandemic that we call COVID.

We are all, in so many ways, from the same womb, and this should lead to a common experience of humanity that does not leave anybody behind. But in the reality of life, some are left behind along the roadside, left behind in culture, behind in development, behind in incomes, behind in outcomes. All kinds of experiences separate us and make us unequal and uneven. So, let us consider this pandemic a wake-up call. Let us go look for our brothers who are discarded and left behind. Let us go look for our sisters who have been abandoned. Let us go look for the men and women whose absence makes us feel less whole and less wholesome, and bring them all together, and make real the unity of the human family.

A Wave of the Hand.
A Nod of the Head.

Loretta Claiborne is a multisport Special Olympics athlete and recipient of the 1996 Arthur Ashe ESPY Courage Award.

ᘓ

P eople are experiencing social isolation today like never before, but people with intellectual disabilities experience it all their lives. At home, I was always in the thick of things, but when I stepped out of my door, I was socially isolated. I had no connection. But I was blessed. In high school, someone told me, "Loretta, I think you are going to like this." It was Special Olympics, and she was right. I started in 1970, and it's the best thing I've ever done. We talk about being separated, but when I come together with my athlete friends, we're all connected. People volunteer at the program, thinking they are going to teach us because we have an intellectual disability. But we end up working hand in hand and teaching each other.

We have to learn more about others. When I went to the Special Olympics World Games, I had a little dollar-store watch, and I gave it to an athlete from Iraq. The United States was fighting with Iraq at the time. We didn't even know if she was going to get home safe, and here I was talking a few Arabic words to her and giving her a watch. I opened her world. She opened mine.

If we could just take a couple of seconds of our time when we see somebody to say "hi" with a wave of the hand or a nod of the head—that makes a difference, and starts to unite people. One way I've been doing that in my spare time, and way before the isolation from COVID-19, is by knitting little preemie caps that are sent to hospitals. Three different hospitals: one in Pittsburgh, one in North Dakota, and, of course, my own hospital where I was born. Any mother in one of those hospitals who has a baby that's premature gets one of my little caps. I'll never see one of those babies, and I'll never meet one of those mothers, but I know I'm doing something for mankind. You don't need to do things like that, though. How about a smile? A wave of the hand or a nod of the head? If you smile, wave, and nod your head to someone on the street, you can open up a world.

Sports instructor Marina Cruz motivates Pilar Zanon at the ALAS Foundation center for women with intellectual disabilities. Madrid, Spain. June 2020.

One Family. One Love.

Sean "Diddy" Combs is a rapper, singer, writer, record executive, producer, and actor.

❧

Since the coronavirus began, we have been quarantined at home, and it's given me time to reflect on things I wish for. And one of my greatest wishes is for us to unite as one global family and stop the injustices that are happening to our extended family, our brothers and sisters, people of color, minorities. I pray for the day that we come together united in love. We don't have to wait until the pandemic is over to unite. This dream could come true right now, as it *has* been coming true. We *are* getting more united. So today or tomorrow, be kind to someone. Give somebody an extra mask. Check on an elderly neighbor. Let's stay united. One family. One love.

Determined to Rise

George W. Bush served as the forty-third president of the United States from 2001 to 2009.

❧

This is a challenging and solemn time in the life of our nation and world. A remorseless, invisible enemy threatens the elderly and vulnerable among us. A disease that can quickly take breath and life. Medical professionals are risking their own health for the health of others and we're

*Medical workers at a nursing home severely
impacted by COVID-19. Albino, Italy.*

deeply grateful. Officials at every level are setting out the requirements of public health that protect us all, and we all need to do our part.

The disease also threatens broader damage. Harm to our sense of safety, security, and community. The larger challenge we share is to confront an outbreak of fear and loneliness, and it is frustrating that many of the normal tools of compassion—a hug, a touch—can bring the opposite of the good we intend. In this case, we serve our neighbor by separating from them. But we cannot allow physical separation to become emotional isolation. This requires us to be not only compassionate but creative in our outreach. And people across the nation are using the tools of technology in the cause of solidarity.

In this time of testing, we need to remember a few things. First, let us remember we have faced times of testing before. Following 9/11, I saw a great nation rise as one to honor the brave, to grieve with the grieving, and to embrace unavoidable new duties. And I have no doubt, none at all, that this spirit of service and sacrifice is alive and well in America. Second, let us remember that empathy and simple kindness are essential, powerful tools of national recovery. Even at an appropriate social distance, we can find ways to be present in the lives of others to ease their anxiety and share their burdens. Third, let's remember that the suffering we experience as a nation does not fall evenly. In the days to come, it will be especially important to care in practical ways for the elderly, the ill, and the unemployed. Finally, let us remember how small our differences are in the face of this shared threat. In the final analysis, we are not partisan combatants. We are human beings equally vulnerable and equally wonderful in the sight of God. We rise or fall together and we are determined to rise.

In the Locker Room at Halftime

Darrell Green is a former NFL cornerback and Hall of Famer.

⤳

I pray to God that not one of us will exit this time of crisis in the same way that we entered it.

I want to urge us to unite with one another, and more importantly, to take this moment to unite with God. My desire to draw near to God starts off with repentance. God, please examine me and know me well and make me better.

We start there. We repent. This isn't a time-out. This is halftime. We're in the locker room at halftime, going over the game and getting our plan as we go back on the field, back on the road to navigating life.

But we're going to be navigating life in a new way, where love and concern for our fellow man and obedience and patience and kindness and gentleness and faithfulness will be the mark of the day. The world after us will know that this time happened because of the love that we have for one another.

I encourage everybody—please, please, please—I plead with you: do not exit this time in the same spiritual way that you entered it. Give us, give yourself, give God, and give the world your commitment to that.

It is my extraordinary privilege to say to you I love you.

I Pray We All Heed the
Call to Unite

*His Holiness the fourteenth Dalai Lama is a Buddhist monk and
the spiritual leader of Tibet.*

∽

I n this time of crisis, we face threats to our health and sadness for the family and friends we have lost. Economic disruption is posing a major challenge to governments and undermining the ability of so many people to make a living.

It is during times like this that we must focus on what unites us as members of one human family. Accordingly, we need to reach out to each other with compassion. As human beings, we are all the same. We experience the same fears, the same hopes, the same uncertainties. Yet we are also united by a desire for happiness. Our human capacity to reason and to see things clearly gives us the ability to transform hardship into opportunity.

This crisis and its consequences serve as a warning that only by coming together in a coordinated global response will we meet the unprecedented magnitude of the challenges we face.

I pray we all heed the call to unite.

When Their Story Becomes
Your Story

Pastor Judah Smith is the lead pastor of Churchome, formerly called The City Church. He is the New York Times*–bestselling author of* Jesus Is _____.

∽

My passion is to follow Jesus and tell the story of Jesus to the world, of the love and grace he demonstrated through his life. He was constantly sharing meals with others, which was one of the most intimate acts in antiquity, and he did that with the marginalized. He did that with those said to be nonhumans. He did it with women and children, which in his landscape was unheard of. He was a revolutionary, and I love him and look up to him and want to follow him.

So in our home we are practicing being a good neighbor. What does it mean to be a neighbor, which was paramount in the teachings of Jesus? For me, it has landed on loving your enemy. In these times, that calls us to be less cantankerous, less contentious with our public figures who are doing the best they know how. We need to offer love, respect, honor, and dignity to each person represented in public office.

Loving your enemy also means coming to know the people you overlook— the people you don't really see. It is a learning curve. It means learning how to have meaningful conversations, with each person taking time to share their thoughts while the others in the conversation quiet themselves, offer eye contact, and engage in what they are hearing. It's saying to others, "Tell me your story, tell me your pain, tell me what you're suffering, what you are going through."

I feel we have an opportunity right now to do what I like to call "stay in the story." The story of humanity is being played out all around us, and it is not just my story or your story or their story. It's our story. It belongs to all of us. And to listen to another man or another woman's story is to add depth and dimension to your story. And when their story becomes your story, you begin to experience true love and true empathy and true compassion, and that changes the course of the world.

Everybody Is a House of God

Reverend Dr. Jacqui Lewis is the first African American and first woman to serve as senior minister of Middle Collegiate Church in New York City.

⁓

Our church is a 1,300-member multiracial, multicultural, multiethnic, many gendered, all sexual orientations, fully welcoming, wild and wonderful congregation that loves art and loves justice. And I am a Christian pastor who, unsurprisingly, believes there is more than one path to God. When I say that, though, I sometimes get hate tweets. "What? Jesus is the only way, the truth and the life!" When I was a younger Christian, I believed that. But now, as I've grown up and as I've moved in the world with so many amazing multifaith leaders, I'm crystal clear that God speaks more than one language. God wants all of us to belong to God, and God, I believe, is love.

There is a little text in the Christian Bible that says, "God is love, and those who live in love, live in God, and God lives in them." You know what that means? Everywhere love is, God is. In a family taking shelter at home. Between partners, lovers. Between a mother and a child. Between neighbors who knock on the door and say, "Can I bring you groceries?"

God is love and everywhere love is, God is. That means all of us who love are love shacks. We're all houses of love. So, I think we have a chance to both simplify our faith and amplify our faith at the same time. What if all of this religion stuff is just about loving each other? What if we don't have to fight about how to call God? What if we don't have to make people pass a test before they can join a church? What if all we have to do is treat each other like God is in each of us?

Imagine everybody houses God. Everybody is a house of God. God lives in them. And love is where God is and God is where love is. If we bind ourselves around love, we can not only get through this crisis, but we can make the world a place of peace and joy where we all love our neighbor and everyone has enough.

The Reason I Love

Common is a rapper, actor, writer, and founder of the Common Ground Foundation, which provides mentorship to high school students.

∽

I have been spending some time alone, watching movies, praying and meditating, exercising, listening to music, talking to friends. Some days I just sit and do nothing, just looking at the trees, appreciating life. And when I was thinking about what a call to unite means to me, I started to contemplate

*Kim Soto and her daughter give each other a kiss as they
play in the water. Voorhees, NJ, USA. July 2020.*

what really is the word *unite*? What does it mean? What is the core of it? And the thought that came to my mind is love. To unite is to love. But where is love? Where can I find it?

I find it in the laugh of my grandmother
when she told me she couldn't get her nails done.
It's the reason I love being her grandson.
I find it in a stillness as these days move slow and fast,
the more I'm still, the more I know what to grasp.
I find it in letting go of what I used to do every day
and now a new born gratitude is what I choose every day.
I found it in my daughter, asking me, "Is dude being truthful?"
Love is listening. I gotta tell her the truth though.
I felt love in the death of my friend Jamie who grew up around 87th
*   with us.*
There's a beauty for ashes that was ashes to dust.
There was love even in the loss, and what I found is they never leave
*   us completely.*
The pieces of their spirits are the things that complete me.
It's in the pastor reminding me we're kings and queens, men and
*   women,*
and we're put on this earth to have dominion, new beginnings.
Yeah, love.
It's in listening to Rakim again, I find it in the Verzuz series by
*   Swizz and Timbaland.*
I must say it's changing me because I'm in quarantine finding love in
*   the club.*

It's nice to deposit into thoughts that are posited. My friends worry
    about dying,
I say, no, man, we gotta live and live well.
We live in happiness, we live in His likeness
because that's where life is, where the spirit and light lives.
We live in happiness, we live in joy,
we live in a peace that only going with them can employ.
We live in a well. Well, we'll call it wellness,
through sickness and ailments the face of faith will prevail us.
We live in abundance with free minds that know how to take care of
    each other.
A care, that generosity and compassion can uncover.
We live in a grace beyond what we can fathom,
overflowing dreams we have them,
flowing from streams of passion,
a calm that was described before we took physical form
and our work will be love. Shout out Kahlil Gibran.
We live in a hope that rises above old fears,
a forgiveness that clears away old tears.
And we can be in a state of eternal love for whole years.
The sounds of angels is what our souls hear.
The sounds of angels is what our souls hear.
The sounds of angels is what our souls hear.

Answer the Call

Arthur Brooks is the former president of the American Enterprise Institute, a conservative think tank; on the faculty of the Harvard Kennedy School and Harvard Business School; and the author of eleven books, including The Conservative Heart *and* Love Your Enemies.

༄

One of the things I teach at Harvard is a class about happiness. Crazy, right, at the Harvard Business School? But that's what we all want, and the nuclear fuel of happiness is love. One of the things psychologists have found is that the opposite of love is not hatred, it's fear. When I talk to people all over the country, they're actually fearful, and that's what's creating the horrible discomfort that they're suffering from. If you feel fear, the answer is more love.

So I want to offer a couple of ideas on how each of us can improve our lives and improve the world. Here's my first assignment: Every day, I want you to take three little words and have them come out of your mouth to somebody else: "I love you." It's hard for certain people to say, and it's especially hard in certain relationships. But this is an opportunity to say something meaningful to somebody you actually do love. And it's going to have an impact on your brain chemistry—because when you say "I love you," you stimulate oxytocin, which is the neurotransmitter that functions as a hormone that makes you happier. That love will drive out your fear. That's assignment number one.

The second assignment is harder: love your enemies. We are being driven apart in this country by an outrage industrial complex in media and in politics, and it's telling us if we're good citizens and we care enough, we have to show outrage. We have to hate the people who disagree with us. My friends, that is just wrong. That is one of the reasons that we're not as happy as we should be in this country.

It is beautiful to reach out to people you disagree with, and to stand up to people on your own side who are telling you to hate. Remember, when you hate, somebody else is profiting. Somebody else is getting viewers. Somebody else is getting clicks. Somebody else is making money.

It's time for each of us to think about what we can do to bring America together, and the way we can do that is to say: "I love you. I want to listen to you. It doesn't matter if we disagree about politics." If we can do that, you know it's a new day. If you have fear, you need more love. To love is to answer the call.

*National Health Service workers applaud at St Mary's
Hospital during the Clap for Our Carers campaign.
London, UK. April 2020.*

Epilogue

Maria Shriver

⁓

In early 2020 as the virus began to spread, many of us wondered if we could come out of it changed. Could we come out less alone and more unified, knowing more about what it means to be a whole and complete human being?

In that fearful and hopeful time, an invitation went out, and people from virtually every line of work and walk of life who had deeply thought, deeply felt, and deeply strived came together for twenty-four hours—the honest and the vulnerable, the loving and the courageous, the wise and the wounded, the teachers and preachers and poets and healers who wanted to become better human beings and help us do the same.

They poured out their love to help us feel, ponder, and heal. And from that gathering came a moment-in-time book that will stand the *test* of time—because it shows us that nothing on earth is more lovable and meaningful than humanity taking care of its own.

I hope that in reading this book you felt you were able to pull up a chair, have a seat, and join the conversation, listening to voices of people who sent you their love, showed you their lives, and shared their secrets for making it to safety when the seas get rough. I hope they made you feel less alone, and more a part of the whole.

Mother Teresa famously said, "If we have no peace, it is because we have forgotten that we belong to each other." *The Call to Unite* reminds us on every page that we belong to each other. I hope it helped you enter not just a moment in time, but the *community of our times*, and made you say to yourself, "Here is a home for me. Here is a community where I belong. I may not have found it where I expected it, but I'm excited to be a part of it—and I didn't even know it was here."

The people in our new community give me hope that the division we're seeing in society is not a trend; it is a *reaction* to the trend, and the trend is toward unity, not division. Yes, times are disruptive. But I challenge any doubters to show me a society that has done better with more diversity at a time of greater change. Disruption is a sign of hope. It's the price of honoring our promise to leave the past and lift every voice. And the people guiding us are giving us a new story and a new identity: We are uniters.

The two most exciting things to me about *The Call to Unite* are the community of uniters that is forming around it, and the fact that *The Call to Unite* is the first book of my new imprint, The Open Field. The Open Field will give a bigger voice to the writers and readers of this book and all the architects of change who are building the world of their dreams.

My goal is to publish books that honor one of the most unifying truths in human life: We are all seeking the same things. We're all seeking dignity. We're all seeking joy. We all want to be seen, to be valued, to be understood, to be loved. And here is the miracle—even though we all want the same things, there doesn't have to be any competition among us, because the things we want are not material goods; they are spiritual gifts. We don't need to fight over them, because the supply is infinite. We don't have to battle for them, because when we get them, we can't help but share them. The more love I receive, the more love I give. The more those around me feel joy, the more I'm surrounded by joy. We are not separate. We are one.

My whole life has been a search for this oneness—to unite my interior self with my exterior self—and *The Call to Unite* gives words and direction to my search.

A few years ago, I closed one of my books with a chapter on the power of reevaluating. I had realized that so many of the beliefs and opinions I adopted long ago no longer held up for me. And because some of my biggest moments of growth have come when I realized I was wrong and admitted it to others, I wrote page after page about things I got wrong: beliefs about marriage, the Catholic Church, politics, divorce, addiction, therapy, men, motherhood. But now I realize that there was one thing I left off my list. It was part of every item in there, but I never named it directly.

I was wrong about happiness. And that's not just my mistake. It's ours. I think we have all been massively misguided about what it takes to be happy.

It's audacious to make a sweeping critique of human civilization, but here goes: We're hugely gifted in art, music, dance, and literature. We're making gains in engineering, medicine, science, and technology. But happiness is not something we're doing well. In fact, some experts suggest we're getting worse.

Personally, I think we're getting *ready*. Happiness is the next big human breakthrough.

Thomas Keating, the Catholic priest and contemplative, said that to repent is to change the direction in which we're looking for happiness. That makes sense to me, because the way many of us are seeking happiness is driving us apart. Most of us are seeking happiness in success, and what we're calling success is being rich, or famous, or powerful, or popular. But these are all comparative measures. We can't be rich, powerful, famous, and popular unless others are poor, weak, obscure, and disliked. It locks us into a system where others have to fail for us to succeed. We have to redefine success so it aligns with our natural state, which is unity. That's where we'll find happiness.

If we work just as hard to come together as we've worked in the past to stay apart, we may finally find our destiny as a large, powerful, loving family finding its meaning in helping each other.

This movement toward unity has been quickened by the virus—at least it has for me. At the time of the lockdowns, as the danger became real, many of us were anxious and scared. I know in my own life when I've felt scared, I've been helped most when I've reached out, and someone on the other end has picked up the phone and answered my call.

So much darkness gets cured when we connect with other human beings. That's when we feel whole. My brothers and I were raised to go out and conquer Mount Everest, to be successful in the world, but I've learned the hard way that what makes me whole is one-on-one human connection—when a friend and I can tell each other our stories, share our joy and pain, and help each other toward happiness. That brings me the peace that I thought the bestselling book would give me, that I thought anchoring a show could give me. Human connection is what fills my heart and makes me whole. *That's* when I feel community, and I'm coming to learn that this community is so much bigger than I thought it was.

People have said to me that all this talk about kindness is going away when the virus is over, that everyone's going to go right back to where they started. I don't think so. I'm never going back. I'm a uniter.

Music and Dance from
The Call to Unite

℘

When a visual event is turned into words, something is gained and something is lost. We get a book we can hold in our hands, give to our friends, leave on a dresser or read in our bed. But we lose the joy of listening to music, hearing a voice, or seeing the face of the person performing.

So, as we acknowledge the contributions that created this book, we want to honor the people who appeared in The Call to Unite Livestream Event, which you can still see in full on www.facebook.com/thecalltounite, including these precious moments of music and dance whose power was impossible to convey on a page:

The incomparable **Alvin Ailey American Dance Theater**, who opened the event; the legendary **Quincy Jones,** who introduced the singer **Sheléa**—who sang "You've Got a Friend"; the cellist-genius **Yo-Yo Ma,** who played "Appalachian Waltz"; master choreographer **Debbie Allen,** who gave us a dance lesson sweetened with love; actor **Rob Lowe,** who presented a song by Global Scribes; Rapper **Joseph "Rev. Run" Simmons,** who performed "Sucker MC's," the first record he ever made; **Lil Buck,** who made a stage of a public street and danced to the music of "The Dying Swan"; **Youssou N'Dour,** the Senegalese legend who sang his own call to unite; **Josh Groban,** who played the piano and sang his song "Granted"; the **Kung Fu Nuns** from Nepal, who gave us a martial arts display; **LeAnn Rimes,** who played her piano by the fire and sang "There Will be a Better Day"; and Iranian-American guitarist **Shahin Shahida,** who played his song "Windy Nights" and recited Saadi;

    Michael Israel, who painted a canvas to the sound of music; **Hunter Hayes,** who played his songs "Still" and "Madness"; **Nejla Yatkin,** who danced at Chicago's Lincoln Park conservatory; **Jewel,** who played guitar and sang her song "Grateful"; **Nikodimos Kabarnos,** whose deep Byzantine chanting shook our souls; **Bebe Winans,** the gospel and R&B singer, who sang his song "Humpty Dumpty"; **13 HANDS, aka DALIEN,** who played the Native American flute; **Drew Dollaz,** who danced for us on a rooftop; **Darlene Love,** who sang "Lean on Me" with medical staff from St. Joseph's Health Mission; **Avril Lavigne,** who sang her song "We Are Warriors"; **Israel Houghton and Adrienne Bailon,** who sang their song "Be Still"; **Estelle,** who sang her song "Conqueror" with The Alumni Ensemble of Harlem; and **Tami Pyfer,** member of the Tabernacle Choir at Temple Square, who sang "Love at Home" with her husband, Aaron, and their five children;

    Opera singer **Joyce DiDonato,** who sang Reynaldo Hahn's "À Chloris"; **C5 Artists,** who performed their original dance "Retrouvaille"; **Andrew Bird,** who played guitar and sang his song "Take Courage"; **Huang Yi Studio +,** who performed a dance meditation on connection—with a robot; **Alphabet Rockers,** who rapped their original song "On the Corner"; **Andrew Adams,** who performed an aerial dance with an umbrella; **Jon Boogz,** who danced to Bach on the beach; **Chloe and Maud Arnold,** who tap danced in a park in Los Angeles; **Ally Brooke,** who sang her song "Perfect"; **Mandy Moore and Taylor Goldsmith,** who performed their song "Silver Landings"; **98 Degrees,** who sang a medley of their hits; **Richie Cannata,** who played a saxophone solo of "New York State of Mind"; **Young People's Chorus of New York City,** who sang "Give Us Hope"; **David Broza,** who played his song "YiHye Tov (Things Will Get Better)" and The **African Children's Choir,** who sang "Amazing Grace" and "He's Got the Whole World in His Hands";

Rodney Atkins, Rose Falcon, and their baby Scout, who sang "Figure Out You"; SOFI TUKKER, who played their song "House Arrest"; Lyla June, Millicent Johnson, Jade T. Perry, Alexis Francisco, Marcia Lee, Teresa Mateus, and Aarthi Tejuja, who called on us to listen to the voices of Black, Indigenous, and People of Color who are feeling the effects of this moment in disproportionate ways; Asher Angel, who sang his song "Guilty"; Filastine & Nova, who sang from the Pacific Ocean; Filipina American rapper Ruby Ibarra, who performed her song "Someday"; the Choir of the International School of Kuala Lumpur, who sang "North" by Sleeping at Last; the spiritual healer Gogo Dineo Ndlanzi, who sang and preached; actress Amandla Stenberg, who played the violin; Le Patin Libre, who displayed their performance art of "contemporary skating"; beatboxer, rapper, and producer D-Nice, who was DJ for our around-the-world Purpose Party; Kodi Lee, who played the piano and sang "Keep Your Head Up"; Malaysian singer Yuna, who performed her songs "Deeper Conversation" and "Lullabies"; and ten newborn babies—some of them already singing—who came into the world during The Call to Unite in the Paropakar Maternity and Women's Hospital in Kathmandu;

Peter Yarrow of Peter, Paul and Mary, who played "Puff, the Magic Dragon"; singers from Parkland's Marjory Stoneman Douglas High School, who sang "Shine"; Rodrigo y Gabriela, who played their song "Diablo Rojo" on guitar; Nigerien singer-songwriter Bombino, "the Hendrix of the Sahel," who played his song "Imuhar"; young Muslim woman hip hop artist Mona Haydar, who "knocked 'em out the box" with a spiritual rap; bestselling gospel singer CeCe Winans, who sang "Count on Me"; Aloe Blacc, who sang "Love is the Answer" and "Wake Me Up"; seven-year old Greek piano prodigy Stelios Kerasidis, who performed his composition "Isolation Waltz"; vocal trio GENTRI, who sang their song "Believe"; SoHyun Ko, the thirteen-year old violinist, who played Paganini; DJ Jazzy Jeff, who got everyone up to dance; producer and rapper Questlove, who brought us to the end with seventy-nine songs in six minutes; and Michael Stipe, lead singer and lyricist for R.E.M., who closed the show singing his song "No Time for Love Like Now."

Each one of these performers, including the newborns in their first day of life, contributed an essential piece of the power of the twenty-four hours that prompted people to say, "This should be a book," even if everyone couldn't be in it. Their singing and playing and dancing, and the joy they inspired in us, are proof of the oneness that underlies all difference. We thank them all.

Participants in The Call to Unite
24-Hour Livestream Event
April 30–May 1, 2020

⌒∽

98 Degrees, African Children's Choir, Alan Lightman, Alicia Kettler, Ally Brooke, Aloe Blacc, Alphabet Rockers, Alvin Ailey American Dance Theater, Amanda Kloots, Amanda Lota, Amandla Stenberg, Amy Grant, Andrew Adams, Andrew Bird, Andrew Yang, Angela Faith, Angélique Kidjo, Angie Thurston, Anwar Khan, Archbishop Thabo Makgoba, Arianna Huffington, Arlene Samen, Armstrong Williams, Arthur Brooks, Asha Ramgobin, Asher Angel, Avril Lavigne, Barbara Holmes, BeBe Winans, Biso Tutu-Gxashe, Bombino, Brandy Banaay, Brian McLaren, Brie Stoner, Brooke Williamson, Bryan Stevenson, Byron Katie, C5 Artists, Cardinal Turkson, CeCe Winans, Pastor Chad Veach, Charlamagne tha God, Charli D'Amelio, Chief Roberto Múkaro Borrero, Chloe and Maud Arnold, Chris Miller, Christian Wiman, Common, Courtney Meadows, D-Nice, Dale Pink, Dalien/13 Hands, Daniel Dae Kim, Daniel Wright, Darlene Love, Darrell Green, David Brooks, David Broza, David Gabor, David Lat, David Piña, David Whyte, Dawn Feldthouse, DAYBREAKER, D'Neil Schmall, Debbie Allen, Deepak Chopra, DeVon Franklin, Diana Berrent and Survivor Corps, Diana Winston, DJ Dummy, DJ Jazzy Jeff, Dominique Devezin, Donna Hicks, Donna

Hill Howes, Dr. Antonia Novello, Dr. Ashwin Vasan, Dr. Daniel Douek M.D. PhD., Dr. Dara Kass, Dr. Dawn Brooks-DeCosta, Dr. Elizabeth Mitchell and Dr. Allie Gips, Dr. Enrico Poletti, Dr. Filip Haas, Dr. Lakshmana Swamy, Dr. Mary Leuchars, Dr. Mohamed M. Traore, Dr. Omar Maniya, Dr. Rheeda Walker, Dr. Steven McDonald, Dr. Uché Blackstock, Drew Dollaz, Eckhart Tolle, Elizabeth Gilbert, Ellen Bennett, Estelle, Esther Wojcicki, Eva Longoria, Father Greg Boyle, Father Leo Patalinghug, Father Richard Rohr, Federica Vegas, Filastine & Nova, Fiona Lowenstein, Gabrielle Bernstein, GENTRI, gina Breedlove, Minister Glenda Sherrod, Global Scribes: Youth Uniting Nations®, Gogo Dineo Ndlanzi, Gov. Phil Bryant, H.E. Shamma al Mazrouei, His Holiness Bartholomew I, His Holiness the Dalai Lama, Hope Mutua, Huang Yi Studio +, Hunter Hayes, Hussein Fahmy, Il Volo, Iliza Shlesinger, Imam Omar Suleiman, International School of Kuala Lumpur, Israel Houghton and Adrienne Bailon, Jack Kornfield, Jackie Kinsella, Jane Feldman, Jason Beghe, Jay Shetty, Jeanette Jackson-Gaines, Jennifer Bailey, Jennifer Garner, Jessica Encell Coleman, Jessica Sanchez, Jewel, Joan B., Joe Primo, John Bridgeland, Jon Boogz, José Andrés, Joseph "Rev Run" Simmons, Josh Groban, Jovi Greene, Joyce DiDonato, Judah Smith, Julia Roberts, Kabir and Camille Helminski, Kailash Satyarthi, Kamey Gomez, Kasia Urbaniak, Kate Judge, Kelly McGonigal, Kendal Kost and Charlie, Kerry Kennedy, Killian Noe, Kodi Lee, Krista Tippett, Kung Fu Nuns, Lamont Young, Laura Guanolusia, Laurene Powell Jobs, Lawrence Bartley, Le Patin Libre, Lea Salonga, LeAnn Rimes, Lee Daniels, Leo and Mike Cascioli, Lil Buck, Lindokuhle Nkuna, Loretta Claiborne, Lyla June, Mahdia Lynn, Mandy Moore, Marc Brackett, Maria Shriver, Mariam Mhina, Marianne Williamson, Marie Kondo, Mark Shriver, Mark Updegrove, Martha Beck, Martin Luther King III, Martin Sheen, Mayor Francis Suarez, Meisha Lerato Robinson, Meria Carstarphen, Michael Faye, Michael Israel, Michael Merritt, Michael Stipe, Michelle Arévalo-Carpenter, Mirabai Starr, Mona Haydar, Mujib Mannan, Myriam Sidibe, Nadya Okamoto, Naomi Campbell, Naomi Judd, Naomi Shihab Nye, Ndaba Mandela, Neil Bush, Nejla Yatkin, Nikodimos Kabarnos, Noa Achinoa, Oprah Winfrey, Parkland students, Peace Corps, Peter Gabriel, Peter Yarrow, Philippines Healthcare Workers,

Population Services International, Portugal. The Man, Prajakta Koli, President Bill Clinton, President George W. Bush, Professor Daniel M.T. Fessler, Professor Eyal Leshem, Questlove, Quincy Jones, Rabbi Abby Stein, Rabbi Jonah Pesner, Rabbi Marc Gellman, Rev. angel Kyodo williams, Rev. Jacqui Lewis, Richie Cannata, Rick Warren, Rob Lowe, Robert Glasper, Robert Waldinger, Rodney Atkins, Rodrigo y Gabriela, Roshi Joan Halifax, Ruby Ibarra & The Balikbayans, Rudo Gumbo, Sachem HawkStorm, Sage Robbins, Samantha Levin, Sara B., Sarah Hemminger, Savior Children Foundation in Ghana, Scarlett Lewis, Sean "Diddy" Combs, Shahin Shahida, Shaka Senghor, Shaka Sisulu, Shefali Tsabary, Sheikha Chaica Al Qassimi, Sheikha Intisar Salem Al Ali Al Sabah, Shéléa, Sherri Mitchell, Simon Sinek, Sir Ken Robinson, Sister Norma Pimentel, Sister Simone Campbell, SOFI TUKKER, SoHyun Ko, Sofonias Negussie, Solé Cook, Srinija Srinivasan, Steve Aoki, Susana Lungo, Suze Orman, Swami Atmarupananda, Taylor Goldsmith, TD Jakes, Terri Razzell, Tiffany T., Tim Shriver, Tony Robbins, Trevar Smedal, Tricia Hersey, UNICEF South America, Valarie Kaur, Van Jones, Wanona Satcher, Yang Lan, Yitz Greenberg, Yo-Yo Ma, Young People's Chorus of New York City, Youssou N'Dour, Yuna Zarai, Zabie Yamasaki, Zave Green

Acknowledgments

This book comes from a show that came from a dream. We dreamed that we could share our love and insight at a time of crisis and come out better. We believed that the truths we speak in chaotic times could be valid for *all* times. And we hoped that coming together with similar worries would give us the feeling that we're not alone.

Our dream came true, and we want to offer our lifelong thanks to everyone who was willing to let us publish their words and magnify the number of people who will benefit from your gifts. Among the many who have contributed to this book and our work, there are some we have to single out:

We owe so much to Maria Shriver, who has been an architect of uniting since before UNITE was born. Maria has made it her passion and mission to become the best person it is possible to be, and to bring all of us along with her. Her advice is always a masterful mix of love and candor, her writing a source of truth and growth. She responded to our vision of a major event with all her skill and generosity and became our hidden producer, making twenty-four hours somehow seem possible.

We are deeply indebted to Oprah Winfrey for her energy, her influence, and her guidance. She has made a career of interviewing wise and loving people, and in the process has taught those of us watching how to become wiser and more loving ourselves. If there is anyone in our fractured world who can help us act on our urge to unify, it is Oprah. She's been a uniter since before we had the words to put a name to what she does. It's an honor to work with her.

As soon as Deepak Chopra heard our idea for UNITE, he put us on the air, and on the map. His instant endorsement gave us huge momentum. He was not only "there at the creation"; he *inspired* the creation.

Meisha Lerato Robinson, "the torchbearer," was born to cross boundaries and break barriers and do kindnesses that others would never think of. The Call to Unite event was Meisha Lerato's idea. We will owe her for that, and for everything that flows from it, forever.

Brie Stoner's unswerving vision for The Call to Unite guided us toward the spiritual teachers who will make this book a source of light to countless seekers for years to come.

Andy Ogden, our writer-musician-designer, has managed a continuous, high-speed artistic synthesis of our mission and action in our videos, on our website, and on social media—and has done it with grace and poise, even when he's working on fifteen deadlines while bouncing his baby Owen on his lap.

John Bridgeland, our expert of bipartisan policymaking, has proved it's possible to be kind, gentle, and loving—and still be the no-nonsense mastermind of a global strategy to save millions of lives.

Darius Baxter, who moves from street protests to dinner parties to TV studios and never compromises his values or rations his views, spends all day every day making our work real and relevant for the community partners he gives his life to.

Lamont Young, who was a victim of gang violence as a teen, got a master's degree in counseling, and served as a residential counselor in a homeless shelter during COVID-19, is always pushing us to make change that matters for everyone.

Zac Hill, our big thinker who always anchors his strategy in the sweep of history, manages operations, contracts, business details, and relations with everyone who makes things run. He is irreplaceable.

Mary-Ellen Blair, whose communications strategy is to always say exactly what she thinks, manages a colliding set of calendars and incompatible schedules for a growing number of people, and seems to gain energy from complexity. All of us love her. None of us have ever met anyone like her.

We want to acknowledge the uncountable contributions of Kathleen Shriver, whose indignant response to social injustice inspires all of us, and who is never afraid to stop a conversation when people aren't being clear. From the start, she has worked assiduously behind the scenes to keep us on time, on course, on message, and—most important—on social media.

We stand in awe of the vision and energy of Andrew Mangino, who has never met an idea he didn't make bigger and may be the only genius we know who makes everyone around him feel smarter. Andrew works harder than anyone, is indispensable to everything, and can't ever be found when it's time to take a bow. If he hadn't answered the call, there would have been no Call.

No matter how lofty the vision and sincere the desire, our event and this book would never have come about without the creative genius and practical experience of Jon Klein and Roni Selig. Their gift for seeing what's real in the ideal and helping the spiritual make peace with the practical—*on deadline*—is the talent that made The Call to Unite happen. It's also the gift the whole world needs if we're going to build the future of our dreams.

The team that came together around Jon and Roni did more work in less time with fewer collisions than any group we've ever watched, and many had never even met each other before. Lorne and Emily Green, Joe Talbott, Dusty Heinzmann, and the team at VIVA Creative; Ken Sunshine, Jessica Berger, Charlie Guadano, and the team at Sunshine Sachs; Maria Ebrahimji, Lori Levin, and Joy DiBenedetto from C5; Christina Taylor and her team at TME; and Bettie Levy, Derek Watkins, Louis Upkins, Lainie Strouse, Geoffrey Menin, and Kevin Taylor all brought together a collection of guests who showed us the world at its best.

Todd Dennett and Laura Gross offered us crucial early planning and support. Carrie Kennedy and Dan McIntosh ran production—integrating marketing, programming, fundraising, and the technical side, while Kanya Balakrishna and Meghan Fitzpatrick came in for the final weeks to get us to showtime.

Jesse Dylan, Priscilla Cohen, and the team at Wondros produced some of the most stunning visual experiences of the event, surrounding words with music and photos that captured the meaning and feeling of unity. Their work is pure artistry.

Peter and Jennifer Buffett have a unique place in our heart and history. They were our first backers, and they had the faith to support our vision as it kept getting bigger. None of the people who founded our organization, produced the show, or created this book would have come together without them.

We owe a deep debt to Rockefeller Philanthropy Advisors for nurturing us as a young start-up and for having the patience of Job in supporting the complexity of this project. We also want to thank Rob Freeman and the team at Proskauer Rose, and we're grateful for the vision, creativity, and generosity of Rob Shepardson and his team at SS+K.

Corinne Nevinny and the Radical Relief Fund stepped into a dynamic role during The Call to Unite, offering us opportunities and supporting us with resources of all kinds. Give Directly offered our viewers a chance to act immediately and generously, Tapp offered invaluable technical support and expertise, and our event sponsors reassured us that we could go forward because they had our back—our thanks to L'Oreal, Skoll, Einhorn Collaborative, Jockey, Matt Harris, Rockefeller Brothers Fund, Pure Edge, NoVo Foundation, and the MCJ Amelior Foundation.

We owe so much of the joy of our days to our UNITE cofounders, who've been hearing the call inside themselves since before we all met: Chris Sizemore, Meria Carstarphen, Courtney English, John Bridgeland, Roger Weissberg, Ellie Manspile, Lamont Young, Darius Baxter, Meisha Lerato Robinson, Brie Stoner, Dan McIntosh, Shannon Currie, Timbo Shriver, Elizabeth Weissberg, Andy Ogden, Andrew Mangino, Joel Benenson, Zac Hill, Kanya Balakrishna, Diane Hauslein, Tami Pyfer, Kathleen Shriver, and the students of Unite Atlanta. Every one of you has the audacity to believe we can be part of the force that makes all things new—and the humility to accept delays and detours as part of the journey.

We want to thank UNITE's close advisers, who tell us we're pursuing the unity the whole world is hungry for—Mark Shriver, Bobby Shriver (yes there are a lot of Shrivers in this work!!), Senator Chris Dodd, Andrew Shue, Yuval Levin, Nick Penniman, Tom Friedman, Van Jones, Martha Beck, Arianna Huffington, David Brooks, Rhonda McGee, Charlamagne Tha God, David Sable, Debbie Allen, Deepak Chopra, Arthur Brooks, Killian Noe, Sister Simone Campbell, Loretta Claiborne, Frank Luntz, Donna Hicks, DeVon Franklin, James Comer, Tim Phillips, Chi Kim, Kerry Kennedy, Robert Waldinger, Rick Warren, Minister Glenda Sherrod, Peter Coleman, Dr. Rheeda Walker, Pete Wehner, Scarlett Lewis, Justin Gest, Brooke Anderson, and Mike Gerson.

The book was brought to life by a remarkable publishing team at The Open Field. We want to single out our editor Jeramie Orton, who has cherished the book as much as we have, who brought coherence out of our tendency toward chaos, and who preserved everything lovable while making it readable. Jeramie's love and discipline made this book happen. We also want to thank Brian Tart, whose faith in the book removed all our doubts; Pamela Dorman, whose wisdom at key moments kept us on course; and the entire team who believed we had a book the world wanted to read—Andrea Schulz, Kate Stark, Lindsay Prevette, Shelby Meizlik, Nora Alice Demick, Alicia Cooper, Claire Vaccaro, Meighan Cavanaugh, and Nayon Cho.

Jan Miller and Shannon Marven gave us their guidance in the crucial skill of telling people about the book. It's a matter of art and science, they told us, and they were especially generous in teaching us about both.

We want to thank Tommy Shriver for his wide-ranging editorial assistance; the indispensable Tami Pyfer, who reviewed every draft; and Olivia Eggers, who read every story, saw the flow of the passages, and helped blend the voices into a book. We wouldn't have made it to publication without Andy Ogden, who did soul-stirring work on the photos; Zac Hill, who conquered the business and contract details; and Dan McIntosh, the guru of the impossible, who mastered the challenge of producing a book with ten dozen authors through the mystical skill of befriending people while asking them to do things they hate to do.

We also want to thank our families.

FROM TIM:

To Rose, Joel, Tim, Tamara, Francis, Kathleen, Sam, and Caroline—I will never need to step back from work to spend more time with my family—because my work is a search for what matters most, and that always leads me to you. Thank you for being the soul of every project I work on—and for teaching me over and over that love is what gives life meaning.

To Linda, whose passion for justice and equality has always put her on the verge of selling the house and living in a tent—thank you for your solidarity with every being who draws breath, for your impatience with every form of division and separation, and for your search for truth, which has always inspired mine. You have brought me more love and happiness than I've ever earned, and I will never feel satisfied that I have thanked you enough.

FROM TOM:

To my boys, Nick and Ben, who have done a good job raising me—your pride and independence proved early to me that pressure in relationships backfires. That crucial lesson—which I wouldn't have had the love or patience to learn from anyone else—is the basis of everything I'm trying to understand more deeply now. I can't imagine who I would have become without you, but I wouldn't want to be him.

To Molly, who is so smart in ways I am not—thank you for listening to my ideas, for being my loving skeptic, and for taking a mad gamble thirty years ago and marrying the man who wanted to read you his essays when we were out on a date. You've shown me what it's like to feel absolutely at home on earth—with no desire to be anywhere but exactly where I am. You, and the sound of your laughter, bring me joy.

Finally, speaking for the entire team at UNITE, we are beyond grateful for the inspiration that gave birth to our organization: the people who live their lives as uniters, who cross divides to work with others, who openly share their personal struggles, and strive daily to love their neighbors. They are living their most audacious dreams to prove that we can, too. Our debt to them is unrepayable.

Photo Credits

1. Susana Vera/TPX IMAGES OF THE DAY via Reuters Pictures
2. *Hindustan Times* via Getty Images
3. Scott Olson/Getty Images News via Getty Images
4. Amir Cohen/Reuters Pictures
5. Alexander Hassenstein/Getty Images News via Getty Images
6. Peter Nicholls/Reuters Pictures
7. Mario Tama/Getty Images News via Getty Images
8. *Boston Globe* via Getty Images
9. Spencer Platt/Getty Images News via Getty Images
10. Kerem Yucel/Agence France-Presse via Getty Images
11. Chip Somodevilla/Getty Images News via Getty Images
12. Stephanie Keith/Getty Images News via Getty Images
13. SOPA Images/LightRocket via Getty Images
14. Spencer Platt/Getty Images News via Getty Images
15. Mike Hutchings/Reuters Pictures
16. Scott Olson/Getty Images News via Getty Images

17. Visual China Group via Getty Images
18. Augustin Paullier/Agence France-Presse via Getty Images
19. John Moore/Getty Images News via Getty Images
20. Daniel Becerril/Reuters Pictures
21. Andrew Kelly/Reuters Pictures
22. Adriano Machado/Reuters Pictures
23. NASA
24. *Star Tribune* via Getty Images
25. Joel Saget/Agence France-Presse via Getty Images
26. Stephen Maturen/Getty Images News via Getty Images
27. Kamil Krzaczynski/Agence France-Presse via Getty Images
28. Joy Malone/TPX IMAGES OF THE DAY via Reuters Pictures
29. Josh Edelson/Agence France-Presse via Getty Images
30. Go Nakamura/Reuters Pictures
31. Ueslei Marcelino/TPX IMAGES OF THE DAY via Reuters Pictures
32. Araya Diaz/Getty Images Entertainment via Getty Images
33. Yves Herman/Reuters Pictures
34. Brent Stirton/Getty Images News via Getty Images
35. Picture Alliance via Getty Images
36. Noam Galai/Getty Images Entertainment via Getty Images
37. Susana Vera/Reuters Pictures
38. Piero Cruciatti/Agence France-Presse via Getty Images
39. MediaNews Group/*Reading Eagle* via Getty Images
40. Henry Nicholls via Getty Images